BY ROBERT L. HOLLIS

Feeling Forsaken? The Revelation of God's Love in Your Suffering

The BASICS of Holy Matrimony

Ready for Restoration? The Revelation of God's Plan in Your Surrender

Ready for Restoration?

Ready for

Restoration?

The Revelation of God's Plan in Your Surrender

Robert L. Hollis, Ph.D.

Promise of Love

PUBLISHING

Published in the United States of America.

Title: Ready for Restoration? The Revelation of God's Plan in Your Surrender

Author: Robert L. Hollis, Ph.D.

Publisher: Promise of Love Publishing

ISBN: 979-8-9909486-4-8

Promise of Love, LLC

Cover Design by: Robert L. Hollis, Ph.D.

Printed in the United States of America

to

Roderick, my sage

and

Lynne, my promised land.

Rock bottom can be the fertile ground where

God plants the seeds of your restoration.

-- Robert L. Hollis, Ph.D.

Contents

Author's Notes

This book is intended to provide helpful information on the subjects discussed. It is provided as a set of guidelines and spiritual concepts, not as a formula for prosperity or success.

Bible references use the New King James Version (NKJV) unless otherwise specified.

To protect the privacy of individuals featured in this book, names and identifying details have been altered.

I share this book with you with love and transparency, not to deliver directives, but rather to provide inspired instruction on how to elevate your life.

Ready for Restoration?

Preface

Only a few people know how deeply dark my life had sunk in the wake of my divorce. Fewer still truly understand the depth of my faithlessness in the ensuing seasons of my life. The concept for this book has been rattling around in my head since I authored *Feeling Forsaken? The Revelation of God's Love in Your Suffering*, but as God led me through my own restoration process, this message for you became more clear to me.

When I finished writing *Feeling Forsaken?* I was in such a dark place that I lacked the heart to start writing *Ready for Restoration?* Authoring that first book was therapeutic. It helped me to comprehend my situation and accept hope for a brighter future. However, as I saw my flesh rise above my faith, I realized that despite my misery, I was not ready for restoration.

Being ready is not an epiphanous point in time; it's a gradual, ongoing process. Being ready is not a state but rather a progressive condition that perhaps has more to do with where you've been than where you are. If someone had asked me in my darkest moments if I was ready, they would have received an emphatic YES. However, being ready to be done with the darkness is not the same as being ready to take steps toward the light. Unfortunately, it sometimes takes the harsh reality of hitting rock bottom to earnestly submit to the process.

In the depths of my despair, I could not see the divine orchestration at play. My life felt like a garden overrun with weeds—chaotic, unmanageable, and suffocating any chance for new growth. Each struggle and moment of pain was like a storm, uprooting my sense of self and faith. Yet, it was within this tumultuous soil that the possibility of restoration began to take root. God was preparing me, even when I was unaware, planting seeds of resilience and faith that would one day flourish.

The journey from darkness to light is not straightforward. It is filled with winding paths, sudden drops, and the occasional dead end. My divorce was not just a legal separation but a severing of my spirit. It left me wandering in a spiritual wilderness, convinced that I could make my own way, pave my own path for a road to restoration. Yet, it was in this wilderness that I began to encounter God in ways I had never experienced before. Each step forward, though painful and fraught with uncertainty, was a step closer to the restoration God had planned for me.

This book is a framework of universal principles for restoration that you can apply to your own situations and circumstances. Using my own experiences as a progressive narrative illustrates how God's plan for restoration is intricately tied to your willingness to surrender. Hitting rock bottom is not the end; it's the fertile ground from which profound transformation begins. Your darkest moments become the soil where God's grace can take root and grow. As you read through these pages, you will uncover actionable principles designed to guide you through your own process of restoration. This story is a testament to hope, redemption, and the unwavering faithfulness of God, offering a structured path for your journey toward renewal.

May this book be a beacon of light in your own journey, guiding you from darkness to the brilliant light of God's restoration.

The Key to Reading this Book

Each chapter begins with an account of my own experiences in seeking restoration after my divorce. Transparent and true, I unabashedly share my story with you, illustrating the step of restoration that's covered by that chapter. Going beyond my personal narrative, each chapter then shifts to discuss the restoration step in a broader context, unpacking principles that can be applied universally. Whether you are facing relational challenges, career complications, financial crises, or any other life hurdles, these principles are designed to personally guide you toward restoration. This book provides a versatile framework that supports all areas of your life, empowering you to find renewal and hope in the wake of any setback.

By engaging with each chapter, you will not only journey through my personal path of healing but also discover actionable steps and spiritual insights that you can apply to your unique situation. No matter what specific challenge you face or the goal you aim to achieve, the wisdom within these pages will help you navigate your own restoration journey.

Introduction

Dear Reader,

Having walked the path of restoration, I write this book with humble transparency. It's so easy to get caught up in where you are that you feel the urge to cover up how you got there. Imagine driving up to your dream house within a beautiful neighborhood in a rusty old hoopty. The house is your new home, but you cannot get rid of the car. So, you hide it in a garage around back and throw a tarp over it. If your neighbors don't see it, and if you don't see it, you can begin to forget that you rode to your new home on your struggles. You can lose sight that your dire straits are evidence that God had you all along because there's no way that old jalopy could have gotten you here without a lot of help.

Some of us will pull out a picture of that wreck and wear it as a badge of honor, saying, "Look what I did! Look what I overcame!" This book is not that badge. I used to be one to applaud myself for my own efforts until I realized that such boasting was a delusion of grandeur. I can do nothing... but God.

Our journeys are rarely as pristine as we'd like to present them. The bumps, the breakdowns, the detours—they are all part of the story. It's tempting to showcase only the polished, victorious moments while concealing the grit and grime of the climb. But it's in those messy, unfiltered moments that we truly encounter God's grace and power.

In writing this book, I want to peel back the layers and reveal the reality of my road to restoration, not to glorify the struggle but rather to highlight the faithfulness of God amidst it. My story, with all its imperfections and divine interventions, is a testament to His unwavering presence. I hope it encourages you to embrace your own story, with all its flaws, as a testament to what God can do in a life surrendered to Him.

As you read, you will find that this book does not offer a quick fix or a polished narrative. It's a raw, honest account of falling, failing, and finding faith. It's about recognizing that our most broken places are often the fertile ground where God does His most profound work. It's about understanding that true restoration does not erase our past but redeems it, turning our most painful experiences into powerful testimonies of God's love and faithfulness.

This book is an invitation to journey together through the valleys and over the peaks, to uncover the divine plan that unfolds in our surrender. It's about acknowledging that while we may arrive at our destination battered and bruised, it's the trek, with all of its trials and triumphs, that shapes us into who we are meant to be.

May this book be a guide and a companion as you travel your own road of restoration. May it remind you that you are never alone, that every step, no matter how faltering, is part of God's grand design for your life. And may it inspire you to see the beauty in the brokenness, the purpose in the pain, and the hand of God in every moment of your journey.

With heartfelt honesty and hope,

-Dr. Rob

Chapter 1: I Believe

But the Helper, the Holy Spirit, whom the Father will send in My name, He will teach you all things, and bring to your remembrance all things that I said to you.

-- John 14:26

I believe in God, the Father almighty, creator of heaven and earth.

I believe in Jesus Christ, His only Son, our Lord,

    who was conceived by the Holy Spirit,

    born of the virgin Mary,

    suffered under Pontius Pilate,

    and was crucified, died, and was buried;

    On the third day, he rose again from the dead,

    ascended to heaven,

I Believe

and is seated at the right hand of God the Father almighty.

From there he will come to judge the living and the dead.

I believe in the Holy Spirit,

the holy universal Christian church,

the communion of saints,

the forgiveness of sins,

the resurrection of the body,

and the life everlasting. Amen.

I believe that God loves me.

I believe He is.

I believe He is the only true healer.

I believe His Word is the medicine that heals.

I believe He knows the end from the beginning.

I Believe

I believe He knows me, personally.

I believe He loves me, unconditionally.

I believe He knows better than I.

I believe He has a plan for my life and He will reveal that plan to me if I learn to discern His voice and listen.

We begin your restoration...

We begin this book with these affirmations... actually, it's bigger than that. We begin your healing process with these affirmations because they are the core, the basis, the foundation for the process of restoration.

Chapter 2: Life... as I Knew It

Transparency. There was a time in my process when I thought I needed no restoration. I was good... no, I was great! The devastation of rampant infidelity was years in the past, and I was freshly free of a 21-year oppressive marriage. Cheating was her decision, but divorce was mine. I had come to grips with the facts:

1. Love was long gone from our marriage,

2. It takes two to have a godly marriage and I believed our divergence from Holy Matrimony was irreversible, and

3. I wanted better for myself... I deserved better!

If my walk had been more solid at the time, I would have recognized that last notion of "deserving better" was an indication that I needed restoration. "I deserve better"?

Really, Rob, who told you that?! We often determine in our own minds what's good and what's not, and we use our own measuring sticks to self-determine how we measure up. Eventually, I would get to the realization that if I, a filthy rag, truly got what I deserved, I would already be thrown in Gehenna. Thank God we do not get what we deserve! Although there are mounting signs of end times, we still live in the Dispensation of Grace!

Reflecting on these times, my focus was on me, and that is only to be expected. When in a dark place, you literally cannot see beyond yourself. Likewise, I was unable to see my path because I had not grabbed ahold of His Light to illuminate my steps. Free, ignorant, and blind can feel like being delivered and restored for a moment, but instead, it positioned me for the process of the true restoration I did not know I needed.

In those days, I carried myself with a sense of pride, believing I had conquered the worst. It was as if I had placed a badge of honor on my chest, proclaiming my victory over past pains. Yet, deep down, I was still wrestling with the remnants of hurt and disillusionment. I was a walking contradiction: appearing whole but internally fragmented. The emotional scars from the infidelity and divorce were still gnawing at me, masked by a façade of strength and independence.

One night, as I lay in bed, the weight of my unresolved emotions pressed heavily upon me. It was then that I heard a gentle whisper in my spirit, reminding me of His Word in Isaiah: "we are all like an unclean thing, And all our righteousnesses are like filthy rags; We all fade as a leaf, And our iniquities, like the wind, Have taken us away."[1]   This realization was humbling. It was a stark reminder that my sense of self-righteousness was misguided. True restoration required a surrender, an acknowledgment that my efforts were insufficient without God's transformative power.

In the midst of my self-sufficient delusion, God's grace was quietly at work, laying the groundwork for my eventual restoration. The process was not instantaneous but a journey of peeling back layers, exposing the hidden wounds that needed His healing touch. I began to understand that restoration was not merely about moving past the pain but embracing a profound change in my heart and mind.

---

[1] Isaiah 64:6

As I advanced, I often found myself clinging to Philippians: "being confident of this very thing, that He who has begun a good work in you will complete it until the day of Jesus Christ"[2] This verse became a lifeline, reminding me that God's work in me was ongoing. It was a comforting assurance that despite my shortcomings and the detours I took, He was faithfully guiding me towards wholeness.

Looking back, I see that my declaration of "I deserve better" was not entirely wrong, but it was incomplete. What I truly deserved was not defined by my own standards but by God's unwavering love and grace. He saw beyond my self-imposed limitations and envisioned a life for me that was rich in purpose and divine restoration.

---

[2] Philippians 1:6

In embracing this truth, I started to shift my perspective. My journey was no longer about proving my worth but about aligning myself with God's plan. It was a daily surrender, an intentional choice to seek His guidance and allow His light to illuminate my path. This shift marked the beginning of true freedom, a liberation that came not from escaping my past but from embracing the transformative power of God's love and grace.

Transparency was no longer a fleeting notion but a foundational pillar in my restoration journey. It required a courageous vulnerability, a willingness to expose my weaknesses and invite God's healing into the deepest recesses of my heart. Through this process, I discovered that true strength lay not in self-reliance but in the humility to acknowledge my need for God's restorative power.

In the end, life as I knew it was just the starting point. The real journey began when I surrendered my illusions of control and allowed God to lead me toward a restoration that was far beyond my expectations. It was a journey marked by grace, illuminated by His light, and anchored in the unshakeable truth of His love.

From where do you want to be restored?

We often set our sights on where we want to be without taking account of where we are. Imagine using your GPS navigation to get to a destination without providing a starting point. Sometimes, if you're in an obscure location even GPS will tell you, 'go somewhere where I can start helping you.' Do you know where you are, and are you positioned to be restored?

Keep in mind that restoration and elevation, although potentially related, are indeed two different things. Elevation means getting to a higher station that you have not previously achieved. Restoration means getting back there, and beyond. Job lost wealth, but his headcount of livestock was restored and doubled. Job lost his health (painful sores from head to toe), but was restored to a life of longevity, surviving 140 years after his restoration to

From where do you want to be restored?

see 4 generations of grandkids. And after losing 10 (arguably unruly)* children, Job's family was restored with a great family.

* Unruly children? I say "arguably" because the text does not explicitly label the children as such. However, their regular feasts could indicate a lifestyle of indulgence or lack of restraint, which could be perceived as unruly behavior, especially in contrast to Job's pious character. Job himself seemed concerned about their spiritual well-being, as evidenced by his regular offerings of sacrifices for them, "For Job said, 'It may be that my children have sinned, and cursed God in their hearts.' This Job did continually"[3]. This action implies that Job was worried about their conduct and spiritual state, possibly

---

[3] Job 1:5

From where do you want to be restored?

suggesting they might not have lived up to his own standards of piety and reverence towards God.

So, what about you? Are you trying to return to a station once lost or are you trying to get to a station never before achieved? If the latter, you might already be on the right track. If the former, there may be a Spiritual reason for your fall. In either case, be mindful of the steps and underlying messages of the following chapters.

Chapter 3: Called to Rise

Sometimes you are called in ways that you can hear only if you're ready to receive the call. This was true of my early days of re-bachelorhood. My pastor had been guiding me through every step of my divorce process, never suggesting divorce but highlighting wisdom when I needed it most. God had His grip on me, even guiding me to turn down dates during the final days of divorce proceedings because I was still married. I was committed to starting my next relationship right.

When divorce day finally came, there was no sense of being called. I was set free and ran from nearly everything except myself. Focus on me. Build my life. Enjoy hanging out with friends and casual dates. If I was called, I was not even open to hearing it... until...

Called to Rise

At the end of my first year of re-bachelorhood, I discovered just how insignificant my relationships were. My friends spent the holidays with their respective families. My casual dates had their own families too. And my kids were split between me and my ex-wife for Christmas and New Year's. For the first time in my life, I spent Christmas alone. That awakened me to value deep relationships again. Yes, I was ready for the restoration of my relationship status, or so I thought. As is common for someone seeking restoration, it was all about me. I prayed for God to deliver me into a fulfilling relationship. Restore me so I can be happy. The very premise of the prayer indicated that I was not ready because it was clear that I still could not see beyond myself.

Except for my sister and pastor, I sailed through the divorce process in isolation. This is not a good situation because the enemy does his best work when you're in isolation[4]. Truly, many voices can talk to you and the ones who are guided by His Spirit and grounded in His Word will light a righteous path for you. The ones who are not can lead you into darkness (fear, vengeance, retribution, retaliation), even if they have the best intentions for you. So, during the year following my divorce, I started meeting regularly with a men's group. We called it simply, Men's Fellowship. It's a forum to bring challenges, seek counsel from godly men, and accept accountability to live right and live up to our word.

As I entered into the intentionality of finding a wife, I vented with my men's group about the frustrations of modern-day dating. I had some dates express great interest without much availability to cultivate a

---

[4] Matthew 4:1-11

relationship. Ghosting is real, but in some cases only temporary. I might write someone off for being nonresponsive only to see her come back weeks later. And then there were the overly aggressive women. In one case, my date seemed disappointed that I did not bring an engagement ring to our first coffee shop meet-up! Seeing such a range between non-committal and desperate suitors, I asked my Men's Fellowship, "Why is it so difficult to find a good woman?" Men's Fellowship came through with the perfect answer, in the form of a question... "Have you asked God?"

When called, you're not called into a state of being. You're not called into a station. You are called into service. The Hebrews were not called to just live in the Promised Land; they were called to occupy and serve the Lord. You can see this throughout the Old Testament, particularly in the books of Exodus, Deuteronomy, and Joshua:

Covenant Relationship: The concept of the Hebrews serving and representing God is rooted in the covenant between God and Israel, established with Abraham and reiterated with Moses. This covenant emphasized that Israel was chosen by God not for privilege but for responsibility — to be a "kingdom of priests and a holy nation"[5].

Laws and Commandments: The extensive laws given to the Israelites, detailed in Leviticus and Deuteronomy, were intended to set them apart from other nations, reflecting God's holiness and justice. Deuteronomy[6]

---

[5] Exodus 19:6
[6] Deuteronomy 4:5-8

emphasizes that observing these statutes would show their wisdom and understanding to other nations, thereby representing God.

Warnings Against Idolatry and Moral Decay: Numerous passages warn the Israelites against adopting the idolatrous practices of surrounding nations. For example, in Deuteronomy 8, the Israelites are warned not to forget God when they are satisfied with the wealth of the land. This suggests that their prosperity was intended to enable them to focus more on their spiritual obligations rather than merely enjoying material comfort.

Role as a Light to the Nations: Isaiah[7] speaks of Israel's role as a light to the nations, indicating that their mission

---

[7] Isaiah 42:6, Isaiah 49:6

was to extend beyond their own national boundaries and bring the knowledge of God to others.

Prophetic Calls to Justice: The prophets often called Israel back to this fundamental role when they strayed. For example, Micah[8] emphasizes doing justice, loving kindness, and walking humbly with God, which encapsulates the moral and ethical representation of God in everyday life.

Since the Hebrews were not ready to enter the Promised Land due to their lack of faith, they spent an additional 40 years in the wilderness to mature. But ask yourself, what might have happened had they entered Canaan without God's blessing? We can only speculate, but an example had already been set in the story of Abraham, Sarah, and

---

[8] Micah 6:8

Hagar. Must we be so bold as to chart our own paths to the promises He gives? Must we be so impatient? In my case, yes. Furthermore, I was too focused on getting what I had promised myself that I wildly misinterpreted His answer to my question.

"Why is this so difficult?" I asked in prayer, and within 24 hours I met Elle, who seemed to be everything I was looking for. Unfortunately for me, though, God was answering my question... not answering my prayer. If I thought flaky dates were difficult, God was about to show me the true depth of difficulty in dating without His blessing! Over the following 10 months, He guided me over peaks of glowing joy and through valleys of deep despair to a precipice where I was faced with falling or flying. Devote yourself to her or devote yourself to God. I felt called into Marriage Ministry and reasoned, "If I was with her, I could serve Him better." Problem: Elle was not called.

I thought I was meant to marry Elle; marriage was a common discussion between us. So, I thought this new notion was a sign that we were meant to be. But no, the relationship unraveled as this notion took root in the fiber of my being. I did not just lose the girl, I lost my faith and grew angry with God for answering my question... "Why is this so difficult?" because I was pursuing restoration for my own benefit.

Cornered and Driven into Darkness

It's pretty common for one to press and push to make one's life the way you perceive it should be. As I pressed for my romantic relationship to work out, I also pressed to grow a private business that was not Christ-centered. It was a respectable medical spa and we helped a lot of people lose a lot of weight. Truly, I was proud of our progress and our heart to help, but Christ was not in it. He was not our focus. This was not my calling. So, God called me out of it.

In the natural, there was no tie between the health of my relationship with Elle and the health of my business, but I do accept that there may have been a spiritual incongruence between what I was doing and what I was called to do. As my relationship with her unraveled, my stake in the spa did too. By the end of the year, I was left alone, broken-hearted, broke, and saddled with a mountain of debt from a failed marriage and a failed business. And yet, this was not my lowest point.

Have you been called to a higher station?

Let's face it, we all want to elevate, whether or not we've been in that higher station before, we want to get there now. But is that your desire or His? Is that your will or God's? You can push with all your might, but your rise will be much easier with His blessing.

Less Muscle, More Spirit! If you're pushing too hard to make something happen, ask yourself... Is this what I'm supposed to do? Is this the path I'm purposed to pursue?

Have you been called to a higher station?

Of course, I believe in hard work! Perseverance strengthens you! But, if things that are out of your control are not lining up for you, revisit your "why." Why am I trying to elevate to that station? Why am I pushing this boulder? Weigh your "why" in the light of His Word. Ask Him in submission, "Am I following your heart or merely chasing the desires of my own?" You may be focused on the right destination, but the reasons behind your pursuit may place you on a questionable path to get there. Lock in on God's Word to help you determine if you are truly following Him.

Chapter 4: Refusing the Call

I got it! I was called to glorify God in marriage, not to satisfy myself with marriage. This revelation, coupled with the loss of that relationship with Elle, drove me into rebellion. Like Jonah, I denied God and ran in the opposite direction. But for a year, my whale was more like Captain Ahab's than Jonah's. Finding true love had become an all-consuming obsession. It was the ultimate goal that I believed would satisfy my thirst for the marriage I wanted for myself. My pursuit was marked by futility and despair because true love, my whale, was elusive, defying my efforts to conquer or even comprehend it fully.

I removed myself from all things related to God. No church. No Word. No meetings with my pastor. No guidance from God that I was willing to discern. Even though God is omnipresent, He will not force His way into your heart. That's on you; you control access to your chamber room and He gives you the free will to kick Him out of it.

Consider your heart (an organ of four chambers) to be your inner 'chamber room,' suggesting a deeply personal and innermost part of your being where emotions, thoughts, and spiritual matters are processed and stored. This imagery helps to convey the significance of your heart not just as a physical organ or some fairytale land of feelings, but as the central place of spiritual, emotional, and moral activity.

In the Bible, the heart is frequently mentioned as the site where one experiences deep emotions and desires. For example, Proverbs[9], Jeremiah[10], Matthew[11], and Luke[12] highlight the heart's pivotal role. It's also described as the place where moral and ethical decisions are made, reflecting one's true character and intentions. Proverbs also advises, "Keep your heart with all vigilance, for from it flow the springs of life."[13] This suggests that the heart is a wellspring from which all aspects of life and actions emanate, emphasizing the importance of guarding one's inner thoughts and feelings.

---

[9] Proverbs 27:19
[10] Jeremiah 17:9
[11] Matthew 5:8
[12] Luke 6:45
[13] Proverbs 4:23

Furthermore, the heart as a 'chamber room' implies a private, intimate space where one meets with God. In this sense, your heart is the sacred room where personal communion with the divine occurs, underlining the truth of God desiring a deep, heart-centered relationship with you.

The heart plays a pivotal role in one's spiritual life, and I ushered God out of mine. In essence, I refused His call; I chose to impose my own will over my own life. The story of Jonah is quite popular in children's church because you get to color a giant fish. But as we talk about Jonah's defiance, we can overlook the tempest he brought into his life, and into the lives of everyone around him, because of his refusal to answer God's call. Likewise, rather than accept His sovereign will and His unconditional love for me, I turned from Him and spiraled downward to depths that would affect my family and closest circle of friends.

Adam, where are you?

We serve a God of grace and abundant forgiveness, but we must still face the consequences of our actions. Not all falls from grace are the result of poor decisions. Consider His servant, Job. Are you a Job or a Jonah in your current station? Are you at the nexus of spiritual warfare, or can you recognize the decisions you made that led to the tempest in your life? Can you discern the need for correction in your heart, or have you sunk so deep into the victim mentality that you feel that God and the world have conspired against you?

Reality check, have you ever gotten mad at God for not rescuing you from a situation you created for yourself? Consider the man who drives hard into his career... extra training, company trips, overtime, and being 'the guy' that everyone can count on to pull through. Yes, it feels great to feel so important at work, but the promise of promotion, company car, and large bonuses excite him. By modern measures, he's a great guy, but it has come at the cost of his Spirit Life and Family Life. His church does not know him, his wife feels neglected, and his kids feel ignored. The more she presses for a Kingdom marriage, the more he pulls away with the rationalization "can't you see how hard I work for you?!" Before too long, she stops pressing for his attention and even ceases her suggestions for marriage counseling. "Finally, she gets the picture!" he thought until he saw her across a swanky restaurant one evening while he was schmoozing a new client. She's smiling and laughing with another man as if she had no cares in the world. So free-spirited;

Adam, where are you?

not at all the crab she had turned into at home! He despised her and God for keeping her from realizing how much he does for her. "FIX THIS!", he demanded of God. "I'm sacrificing for her, make her respect me!"

Where are you, Adam?

Is he unable to realize that he created this situation? Does he honestly see all of his accolades at work as a sacrifice? Is he willing to truly sacrifice his desires, die to himself, and love his wife attentively and personally as Christ did for the church[14]? Yes, God can restore this marriage, but is the man willing to turn away from his work treasure to follow and grow closer to God? Is his wife willing to turn away from the comfort she finds in the presence of this

---

[14] Ephesians 5:25

other man? They are both in a station in life that is unsupportive of holy matrimony. These are their respective starting points; realizing where they're starting from enables them to chart a path back to where they once were.

Restoration begins from a place of humility; being humble enough to submit to His guidance and knowing His Word well enough to know His guidance when you receive it. Where are you?

Chapter 5: Sage

Sage (n.): In the tapestry of human existence, a sage is a person who stands as a beacon of wisdom, embodying a profound depth of knowledge and insight that transcends the ordinary. A sage is not merely a repository of facts or an intellectual giant; rather, they are individuals who, through a life of contemplation, experience, and deep connection with the divine, offer guidance and clarity to those navigating the complexities of life.

A sage's wisdom is often marked by humility, compassion, and an ability to see beyond the surface, revealing truths that elude the untrained eye. Their counsel is sought not just for their intellectual acumen but for their spiritual depth and the sense of peace they emanate. In many traditions, sages are revered as spiritual

Who is your mentor?

mentors, guiding souls towards enlightenment and deeper understanding of the divine mysteries.

One of the crucial considerations in starting a new relationship is the condition of your heart. Never date the hurting, and never date while hurting. Healing must come first, and the only true healing comes through Christ. I was in trouble. I had turned from Christ, I was hurting deeply, and I had given up. Absent from church for five months, I was highly susceptible to even the mildest seduction and fell prey to the most ungodly relationship of my life. I tried to will this relationship with Mara into what I wanted it to be, but a patchwork of happy moments covered the holes on my heart, keeping me from realizing my need for mending. Friends and family grew distant as they recognized the darkness consuming me. They tried to help me see the storm that had become my life, but as I stood in defense of this relationship, I kept my back to it, unable to see the tempest for myself. Without facing it, without acknowledging it, it was not possible for me to take ownership of why it was happening. It was not until all of those voices quieted that I turned around, saw my relationship with Mara for what it was, and realized... "I don't want to marry you."

In the weeks prior to this revelation, my in-person friends had dwindled dramatically. About the only one left was my pastor, but we go way back. He started discipling me long before I realized that's what he was doing. Jesus saved me, but this Brother showed me the way to Him. Gently. Patiently. Compassionately. So, this relationship of mine had to make him feel disappointed. Even when he and his wife sat me down and offered to help me dig out of this darkness, I turned them down and declared that I wanted to continue living in darkness. Even with as heartbreaking as that must have been, he never gave up. He just changed his tactic.

First, he stopped attacking my relationship with Mara, and that allowed me to stop defending it. Next, he gave me space to see with my own eyes what everyone else around me had been seeing. And although he released me to my rebellion, he never cast his Brother out of his heart. So, when I asked to meet with him, I was willing and ready to receive his sage advice.

Our common meet-up was a bar of all places, where he would engage the staff and ask to pray for them. He often found a kindred Brother in Christ or someone searching for answers that life had not delivered. It was a fitting place for the lost to meet a Man of God. I don't know why

Who is your mentor?

I requested his presence, I just remember having an air of feigned confidence. I knew he did not approve of my path and a big part of me wanted him on my side. As is human nature, when you want your point to be received, you tend to overtalk it. He saw right through that. He saw right through me and asked, "Rob, why are you doing this?" I was ready for that question! I may have even been subconsciously baiting him into asking it because I was so prepared. But as I opened my mouth to release my rehearsed response, the words would not come out. I sputtered and spun my wheels, like a car trying to get unstuck. I backed up and tried again. I could not speak. Instead, I broke down. I sobbed, no, I flat-out cried my eyes out until I could recite the new response that struck me in that moment: "Because I will never love anyone like I loved Elle. So, I might as well be with someone who loves me like that."

Who is your mentor?

Although I'm sure he provided many great words of wisdom and guidance at that moment, I only remember a few, and a few words were all I needed: "Elle did not just hurt you; she damaged you."

Downtrodden. Damaged. Broken. This is a horrible place to be, but it was exactly where I needed to be. Sometimes it takes the humility of being broken to fully submit to His will and His guidance. The beauty of hitting rock bottom is that now you can bounce.

Who is your mentor?

You can get to a point in your process where you feel like you've seen enough that you know what to do now. "I got this." Typically, Western cultures like the United States and parts of Europe tend to value individualism highly. This trait emphasizes personal freedom and autonomy, leading to a more pronounced reluctance to being told what to do. In societies that stress individual rights and personal achievements, there is a stronger tendency for individuals to resist external control and directives. These societies often foster a sense of independence from a young age. Here's the rub, we do not mind receiving advice when we ask for it, but unsolicited guidance often results in discomfort or defiance. This reflects a basic psychological principle where individuals value their freedom to make choices and may perceive unsolicited advice as an infringement on their autonomy, leading to a defensive reaction, commonly known as "reactance." Often, this reluctance is a reflection of your pride; you may want to prove that you can do this yourself, or you may think you simply know more than the mentor. If you do know more than your mentor, you've chosen the wrong person to guide you.

Keep in mind that a mentor and a coach take different approaches to help you. Think of a mentor like someone who has walked the path you're aiming to tread. They're showing you the ropes, giving you that insider knowledge and wisdom that comes from years of experience. It's personal, often a long-term commitment, rooted in who you are and who you aim to be.

Who is your mentor?

Now, on the flip side, a life coach, they're more like your strategist. They're not necessarily in your field and they may not be able to play the game as well as you, but they know how to push you to your personal best. They work with you on specific goals, short-term plans, professional skills. It's less about who they are and more about what you need to do, right here, right now. They're the ones helping you play the game right, while a mentor, they're more about helping you choose the right game to play.

Is there such a thing as a universal mentor? That depends on who or what you're trying to be. For example, a broke financial advisor is not a good choice for a mentor in financial matters. However, your pastor could very well be a great mentor in Biblical finance.

Who is your mentor?

Whether you pursue a mentor or someone invites you under their wing, get a mentor. Seek someone who knows how to get to where you want to be, be humble, listen, and follow. If you knew how to get to that next station on your own, you'd already be there instead of where you are now.

Chapter 6: Built to Bounce

The Lord is close to the broken-hearted, and saves those who are crushed in spirit.

-- Psalm 34:18 (NIV)

In a world brimming with relentless demands and unending burdens, weariness is a familiar companion. Yet, as followers of Christ, we are inherently designed to bounce back. This resilience stems not from our own strength but from embracing God's boundless power. Let's unpack how leaning on His strength allows us to rise, even when we are utterly exhausted, and understand the essence of resilience in Christ.

We all encounter moments when life's weight presses heavily upon our souls. It's not just physical fatigue but a deep, soul-crushing weariness. Jesus' words in Matthew[15] resonate profoundly: "Come to me, all you who are weary and burdened, and I will give you rest." This invitation illustrates His compassion for us. Jesus also knew the depths of exhaustion. Living among those who constantly sought His healing and wisdom, He teaches us that true strength arises from surrender. When burdened, He invites us to exchange our heavy yokes for His. His yoke is easy, His burden light. Why? Because in Him, we discover the strength to bounce back.

There is unparalleled power in assembling as believers. Like a complex machine that only functions when all parts are in place, we find our true strength when we come together in Christ. Alone, we might feel scattered and ineffective. But together, yoked to Jesus, we can

---

[15] Matthew 11:28-30

achieve the extraordinary. Hebrews[16] reminds us not to forsake assembling together. There is immense strength in unity, especially under Christ's leadership.

Weariness transcends mere physical fatigue; it's a profound exhaustion of the soul. This kind of weariness cannot be remedied with a simple nap or vacation. It burdens the very heart and mind, often exacerbated by life's relentless pressures. Yet, in our weariness, Jesus offers a radical solution: come to Him, take His yoke, and learn from Him. This is not a passive rest but an active partnership.

Your burdens, your cargo can be toxic to anyone who enters your orbit. Even those who try to assist you when you are burdened with such heavy emotional baggage can

---

[16] Hebrews 10:25

find themselves contaminated simply through exposure to you. In 2006, the Probo Koala, a cargo ship chartered by Trafigura, attempted to offload hazardous waste—a mixture of fuel, caustic soda, and hydrogen sulfide—at several European ports, including Amsterdam and Moerdijk in the Netherlands. Both ports rejected the toxic cargo due to its dangerous nature and high processing costs. Subsequently, the ship sailed to Africa and discharged the waste in Abidjan, Ivory Coast, causing severe environmental and public health crises, including deaths and widespread illness. There are people in your life who may wisely keep their distance from you, but the port of Christ will never reject you. He takes whatever burdens that you are willing to release to Him, but just like the Probo Koala would not attempt to take back its caustic cargo, you should not go back and reclaim your burdens once you've laid them at His feet. Exchange that weight for His yoke.

As believers, we are designed to bounce back because we are not meant to carry our burdens alone. Jesus is the ultimate burden-bearer. His invitation in Matthew[17] is not just a call to rest but a call to resilience. He provides the means to carry our heavy loads, making them lighter and more manageable. This does not mean we won't face challenges, but it does mean we won't face them alone.

When yoked to Jesus, He leads, and we follow. Like an experienced ox guiding a younger one, Jesus shares the load and teaches us His ways. This shared yoke symbolizes surrender, companionship, and shared responsibility. It's about moving in harmony with Christ,

---

[17] Matthew 11:28-30

trusting His strength over our own. Jesus' yoke is custom-made for us. It's well-fitted, suitable, and designed to make our burdens easier to bear. His invitation to "learn from Me" is a call to discipleship. It's about adopting His mindset, values, and methods. By learning from Jesus, we discover how to bear life's challenges with grace and resilience.

When life's burdens feel overwhelmingly heavy, remember that you are built to bounce. You are designed to rise again, stronger and more resilient, through the strength of Christ. Embrace His yoke, lean into His strength, and let His grace carry you through.

Your Launch Pad

The journey toward resilience in Christ is an ongoing, transformative process that requires introspection, community, and a deep connection with Christ. As you push through your personal struggles, remember that you are not alone. Jesus invites you to lean on Him, to find strength in His presence, and to draw from the well of His wisdom. Here are some practical steps to help you live out these principles and experience the profound resilience that comes from being built to bounce in Christ.

1. Reflect on Your Burdens

   Begin by identifying the areas in your life where you feel most weary. These burdens might be emotional, spiritual, or physical. Write them down, acknowledging their weight and impact on your soul. Bring these burdens to prayer, laying them at the feet of Jesus. Imagine yourself standing before Him, offering each burden as a gift of surrender. Trust in His promise from Matthew 11[18]. Picture the relief and lightness as you exchange your heavy load for His lighter, well-fitted yoke.

2. Seek Unity in Community

The Christian walk is not meant to be a solitary journey. Hebrews[19] encourages us to assemble together, finding strength and encouragement in our faith community. Engage with your church or small group, sharing your burdens and allowing others to support you in prayer and fellowship. Much like individual threads woven into a

---

[18] Matthew 11:28-30
[19] Hebrews 10:25

tapestry, each believer brings unique strength and perspective, creating a resilient and beautiful community. When you unite with others, you harness collective strength that helps you rise above life's challenges.

3. Embrace Jesus' Yoke

Take time to meditate on Matthew 11[20]. Close your eyes and visualize yourself standing with Jesus, feeling the weight of your burdens. See Him gently lifting them off your shoulders and placing His yoke upon you. Notice how it fits perfectly, tailored to your needs. Reflect on how this exchange shifts your perspective on your struggles. With Jesus' yoke, you are not walking alone; He is guiding you, sharing the load, and

---

[20] Matthew 11:28-30

teaching you His ways. This visualization can be a powerful reminder of His constant presence and support.

4. Learn from Jesus

Immerse yourself in the Gospels, focusing on Jesus' teachings and actions. Observe how He interacted with others, responded to challenges, and demonstrated unwavering faith. Consider how His example can guide you in dealing with your current struggles. As you study His life, let His words and actions illuminate your path, providing wisdom and encouragement. Ask yourself, "How would Jesus handle this situation?" and allow His example to shape your responses and decisions.

By living out these principles, you'll not only find rest but also discover the incredible resilience that comes from being built to bounce in Christ. Embrace the journey, knowing that every step taken in faith brings you closer to the fullness of life He promises. Trust in His strength, lean on your community, and let His teachings guide you. In doing so, you will experience the profound transformation that comes from surrendering to His will and walking in His ways.

Deepen your "Why". Your fellowship with your sage, your mentor may have instilled a deeper sense of purpose. More aligned in your spiritual journey, your "Why" is now rooted in your desire to grow closer to God, to live out His purpose for your life, and to glorify Him in all you do. Let this "Why" be the foundation of your restoration, guiding you through every challenge and triumph.

By understanding and embracing your "Why," you align your actions with your deeper purpose, creating a powerful and unshakable foundation for your life in Christ. This alignment not only strengthens your faith but also empowers you to face life's trials with unwavering confidence and hope. As you continue on your journey, let your "Why" remind you of the greater purpose behind your struggles and the incredible potential for growth and transformation that lies within you. The profound transformation that comes from surrendering to His will and walking in His ways prepares you for the road of restoration more than any human effort or self-driven initiative ever could.

Chapter 7: Crossing the Threshold

I had hit rock bottom long before that talk with my pastor.
My emotional breakdown in the bar that night just opened
my eyes so I could clearly see where I was. I returned to
Mara that evening a changed man. I began to retreat from
her, but she did not see it, or perhaps just did not want to.
The man I had become had the scales removed from his
eyes. I believed in Jesus, or at least the idea of Him, my
entire life. But for the previous nine months, my belief in
Him had waned. What touched me that night in the bar?
Truth! I had already fallen. I was already blinded, but now
the world was different and I knew I had to change my
ways, even if it hurt Mara.

We continued to spend all our time together because, well,
nearly all of my friends were keeping their distance. My

words to end the relationship were unbelievable to Mara. She figured we were just going through a phase. If I could just get over Elle, we would be fine, right? So, she booked a couple's counseling session with a mutual friend and pastor at our church, Ethan. Ethan is the kindest, most gentle man you could ever meet, which is probably why she chose him. He would be on her side for sure! But he had words for us that shocked even me. He said that I definitely needed to heal, and she could not be in my life through that process. "If you care anything for this man, you need to step out of his life." Ethan actually apologized for having to say that, but it had to be said and it had to be done. From that moment on, it still took another two months for her to fully exit my life.

Are you ready and willing to prune?

Consider the process of pruning plant life. Pruning is the process of selectively removing parts of a plant, such as branches, buds, or roots. The primary goal is to remove unwanted parts, improve the plant's structure, and promote healthy growth. Likewise, in life, you may need to prune attachments that adversely affect your walk and impede your growth.

The process of pruning involves:

Timing: The best time to prune is when the plant is dormant and the lack of leaves makes the structure more visible. Likewise, when you are spiritually dormant, it's time to assess what or who is adversely affecting your walk and remove it or them from your life.

Are you ready and willing to prune?

Tools: In pruning plant life, use sharp, clean tools. Similar to needing to make a clean cut from things or people in your life, using sharp tools for pruning plant life is crucial for several reasons, all of which contribute to your health and growth:

Clean Cuts: Sharp tools make clean and precise cuts, which heal faster and more effectively than jagged cuts made by dull tools. Clean cuts reduce the risk of disease and pest invasion. For you, a clean cut keeps the person, people, or activities from influencing you in ways that are unsupportive of your growth.

Reduced Damage: Dull tools can crush or tear plant tissue instead of cutting it cleanly. This damage can stress the plant and lead to weakened areas that are more susceptible to disease and pest problems. For you, the process of repenting is pivoting and turning away from the person, people, or activities that pull you away from Christ. A half-hearted, slow turn can turn you into a pillar of salt as you gaze back at the life you're trying to leave behind. Decide, pivot, eyes forward, and keep moving!

Stress: Clean cuts made by sharp tools help maintain the plant's overall health by minimizing stress during the pruning process. This allows the plant to focus its energy on growth and recovery rather than on healing larger, messier wounds. For you, just rip the band-aid off! A long, slow release from the person, people, or activities keeps you from healing and growing to reach the station you're striving for.

Efficiency: Sharp tools make the task of pruning plant life easier and more efficient. Likewise, the sooner you

Are you ready and willing to prune?

disassociate with the person, people, or activities that hold you back, the sooner you'll get on with your journey. And you do indeed have a journey ahead of you!

Safety: Using sharp tools for plant life is also safer for the person doing the pruning. Dull tools require more force to cut through plant material, increasing the risk of slipping or making an unintended cut, potentially leading to injury. Likewise, if you do not make a clean cut, the bad influence you allow to linger may seek retribution for feeling left behind. "So you think you're better than me now" is a common rebuttal, nicely answered by "No, not better; just different. I'm just in a different place now."

Overall, the importance of a clean cut cannot be overstated. They are key to ensuring that pruning benefits you without causing unnecessary harm or stress.

Are you ready and willing to prune?

You are getting started, heading into an unknown world to face unknown challenges. Divesting yourself of unsupportive encumbrances is crucial to your success on your journey. Jesus told His disciples to leave all encumbrances behind in saying, "Take nothing for the journey—no staff, no bag, no bread, no money, no extra shirt"[21]. Digging into Old Testament Hebrew a little, we can see that Luke was reflecting a principle highlighted by King David: "Yea, though I walk through the valley of the shadow of death, I will fear no evil; For You are with me; Your rod and Your staff, they comfort me."[22] Take a closer look at the word "staff" because it has deeper meaning in this context than meets the eye.

---

[21] Luke 9:3
[22] Psalm 23:4

Are you ready and willing to prune?

David describes his surroundings as a walk through the valley of the shadow of death. Now, David was quite the artist, right? We know he was a songwriter, freestyle dancer, and a poet. As a writer, he was given to using dramatic metaphors, and "walking in the shadow of the valley of death" certainly qualifies.

Shadow of the Valley of Death was originally described by the Hebrew word, salmāwet, which literally means 'the grave', but it FIGURATIVELY means "calamity." So, as I walk through the valley of the shadow of death simply means... as I go through tough times in my life.

OK, so, as I go through those tough times, You (God), are my rod and staff—there's that word, staff—my rod and staff they comfort me.

Are you ready and willing to prune?

What does it mean, in today's terms, when someone 'has your back'? It means they support you, they'll protect you. Well, that word staff is written in the Hebrew text as "mish-eh'-neth," which means a support, a protector, a walking stick. Yes, think about 1000 BC. If I use my biblical imagination, I can see that any walk off the beaten trail was a rough road. You took your walking stick with you to give you stability. Support. Protection from falling. And THAT is what David has to say about our Father... Although I walk on the edge of calamity, I don't fear falling because you're with me God, you are my support, my protection, and you give me stability over the rough terrain of my life.

So, why would you hold onto anything that would hold you back from the One Who will protect and support you through the calamity you're about to face? Yes indeed, on

Are you ready and willing to prune?

your road to restoration, your mettle will be tested. Your character will be tested. Your integrity will be tested. Your faith will be tested. So, prune your baggage and leave it behind.

To truly be ready for restoration, you must be ready and willing to cut your ties to the life you are leaving behind. I cannot express this enough, and if you have any wonder about why this is so direly important, reference the demise of Lot's wife. Lot's wife being turned into a pillar of salt for looking back at the destruction of Sodom is a significant and symbolic event in the biblical narrative. Some interpretations suggest that her looking back symbolized a longing for her former life in Sodom, despite its wickedness and the divine judgment it incurred. This backward glance could imply a reluctance to leave behind the sinful ways of Sodom, highlighting a

Are you ready and willing to prune?

moral and spiritual attachment that was incompatible with the deliverance offered by God.

Do you have such an attachment to the parts of your past that are holding you back?

Lot's wife turning into a pillar of salt can also be seen as a metaphorical warning against regret or yearning for a sinful past when one is called to move deeper into sanctification and righteousness. It serves as a lesson about the dangers of not fully committing to a divinely guided path of escape and transformation.

Are you fully committed to a divinely guided path of transformation? Surely you don't expect to live in the new world as the old you, right?

Chapter 8: Prepare Your Self

When I suddenly set out on this great adventure to restore my love life, like many, I did not gather the tools I would need. I just went. I finally answered my call into marriage ministry as received at the end of my relationship with Elle. One problem though, I was not married! I've come to realize that God does not always call the prepared; He often prepares the called. As with the 12 disciples, Peter recognized that he was unworthy and unprepared[23]. When are we ever truly worthy of doing God's work? When are we ever truly prepared to answer the call?

People often talk about God testing you, and to be honest I never bought into that idea until I traveled this path of restoration. I thought about tests with an academic

---

[23] Luke 5:8-10

perspective. If your teacher wants to know if you have mastered a subject, he gives you a test. But God exists outside of time. Just like you can see all of a painting in one glance, so too can God see all of time in one glance. Knowing the beginning and the end concurrently, He clearly knows how I will perform in any of the tests He gives me! But, the testing is not for Him to learn what I will do; it's for me. It became clear, between Elle and Mara, I clearly was not ready to answer the call.

Tests not only show you your readiness, but they can also show you where you need more work. The interpretation of the test is up to the person being tested. There are those who witnessed me go through some questionable times and have counted me out from ever having a godly relationship because of what they saw. What if I had listened to them? What if I had accepted their perspective? To this day, I am unable to do God's work in their eyes. I call this "The Jesus in Nazareth Effect"[24]. When people cannot see you beyond what you were, it diminishes the depth of what you can be for them now. The most pronounced expression of unbelief I experienced was when someone who knew me since I was a child saw my book *Feeling Forsaken? The Revelation of God's Love in Your Suffering*. Convinced that I was still the ungodly person of my youth, they purchased the book with the sole intent of having a trusted pastor read it and admonish me for being so disrespectful to God. The pastor reported back that it was an excellent book with solid doctrine and great insight. However, despite the positive review, this person from my childhood remains disillusioned about my walk to this day.

---

[24] Mark 6:5, Matthew 13:58

Prepare Your Self

When someone is committed to unbelief,

no amount of evidence will enable them to believe.

I received this experience as another test. When doubted, especially by someone who is deeply important to me, what would rule my emotions? I was actually grateful! You see, I had received wonderful reviews of *Feeling Forsaken?* already, but all were from friends who only knew the new me. They were looking for good stuff, and in life you tend to find what your preconceptions are looking for. In this case, the pastor was sent on a mission to tear the book apart. The stage was set for a horrible review, and yet it still came back positive. Sincerely I say, thank you for doubting me. Thank you for testing me.

The Crab Mentality

Imagine, if you will, a bucket filled with crabs. As one crab determinedly claws its way up the side, nearing escape and freedom, the others reach up and pull it back down. Instead of working together to lift each other up, they hinder one another's progress, ensuring collective stagnation rather than individual success.

This phenomenon is not just about crabs; it's deeply embedded in human social behavior too. It reflects a specific mindset where individuals resent or undermine others' success because it highlights their own feelings of inadequacy or failure. In any social environment where one individual turns to focus on personal growth, this mentality can be toxic. It breeds an atmosphere of competition instead of cooperation, of jealousy instead of joy at others' achievements.

Why do people exhibit crab mentality? It often stems from a scarcity mindset—a belief that success is a zero-sum game, that there is not enough to go around. When someone else's light shines brightly, it feels as though it casts a shadow over their own achievements. This explains part of the reason why pruning is so important. People who feel threatened by progress will intentionally or unwittingly try to derail you. Pruning does not mean you go it alone; I encourage you to surround yourself with uplifting people and look for ways to uplift them too.

When you encounter crab mentality, it may be a reminder that you did not do a thorough job pruning. Pruning does not necessarily mean cutting your loved ones out of your life. However, they do not need to know all the details of your mission, or even that you are on a mission at all. You were called; they were not. So don't hold it against them if they do not understand. As friends, as family, we have a choice. We can be crabs in a bucket, or we can be ladders for each other's ascent. For those who doubt you today, you may be able to be uplifting for them tomorrow. In the end, it's about not just achieving our own potential, but helping others realize theirs as well. This, indeed, is what makes a community thrive, not just survive.

Gear-Up!

Beyond repenting and pruning, I needed a plan. Throughout the relationship with Mara, my pastor would point out that I was out of process. "You're out of process, Rob." "What process?" I kept asking. "What is this process?" To his credit, he provided some good ideas and foundational principles. However, after four decades of unsuccessful relationships, I did not trust myself to ideas and principles; I needed a process! During that year of re-bachelorhood I found quite a few 'get the girl' or 'get a date' processes. They would also teach you how to be a modern-day Casanova. Sounds great, right? Well, do you realize that Giacomo Girolamo Casanova was an Italian author who had (or at least wrote about) more than 120 romantic adventures? To put it bluntly, he was a womanizer. Pop culture seems to have dropped the negative connotation and replaced it with "a man who is good with women." Although Casanova is considered to be a great success in love, those who have studied his life note that he seems to have had only one true love, Lucia. She broke his heart at age 17 and all the other romantic adventures may have been only to mask the pain of the broken heart he never got over. That is not success. I did not want shallow dates. I was not trying to find a girlfriend. I was trying to find a wife! So, after that year of searching and months of asking my pastor for a process, I realized I was looking in all the wrong places. So, as Men's Fellowship suggested two years prior, I asked God. What is the process for finding a wife?

I thought I was asking a simple question, but when you think about the Bible, you got two kinds of instructions God gives: simple and complex.

First up, simple instructions. Take Noah, for example. God tells him, "Build an ark." It's straightforward – he gives Noah the dimensions, the materials to use, who to bring. But the core of it? "Build an ark, survive the flood."

Simple to grasp, but not necessarily easy to do. That's Genesis 6 for you.

Then you got Adam. In Genesis, God tells him, "From any tree of the garden you may eat freely; but from the tree of the knowledge of good and evil you shall not eat." This is a direct, simple command. It's clear-cut, but as we know, even simple instructions can be tough to follow.

Now, on the flip side, you got complex instructions. Think about Moses. In Exodus, God lays out the laws, the tabernacle details, the rituals. It's complex. These instructions come with layers, details, specific measurements, and procedures. It's not just a "do or do not"; it's a comprehensive guidebook on how to live, worship, and govern.

So, what's the difference? When God gives simple instructions, it's often about testing obedience and faith. It's direct, like, "Do this, don't do that." When He gives complex instructions, it's about building a relationship, understanding His nature, and reflecting His holiness in the daily grind – in how you worship, live in community, and relate to Him.

So you see, whether simple or complex, God's instructions are about guiding us, testing us, and pushing us towards a deeper understanding of Him. It's all about that bigger picture, about staying on the path He's laid out for us. There is no simple answer to "what's the process for finding a wife" because the pursuit of a wife is a process of building and deepening a relationship with God and gradually attaining a deeper understanding of His nature. God took approximately 40 years, from Exodus through Deuteronomy to deliver and define the Law for the Israelites. Now, of course, finding a wife is not nearly as complex as Mosaic Law. Still, I should expect it to be more detailed than guidance on how to score a casual date.

Over the course of nearly 1½ months, I could feel God's encouragement to be still and listen. During that time, I encountered numerous revelations in such splendid detail that I wrote them down, dove deeper, and studied each through the lens of God's word. These instructions came in sequence, detailing how to establish and nurture a great marriage from the very foundation of the relationship. And the first steps were all about my growth, preparing my heart to be ready for His daughter. I stepped back and took a holistic look at this process and called it the *5 Steps*

to Find True Love. I finally had my process, and I was ready to find her… my wife!

Where's your bandana?

Let's think about what really happens during a gear-up montage in a film. It's not just about the action of strapping on a belt, sharpening a longsword, or tying on that bandana. It's about purpose. It's about why. Every hero, before they step into the battle, pauses—a moment of clarity, a moment of preparation. This isn't just about preparing their equipment; it's about preparing their minds. They are aligning their actions with their values, their mission. Why do they fight? Who are they fighting for?

Where's your bandana?

In these scenes, we see a physical transformation, yes, but what's far more compelling is the mental and emotional transformation. It's a visual and visceral representation of commitment. The hero is gearing up not just with weapons, but with conviction. He reminds himself of his 'why', and it is this 'why' that strengthens him, that prepares him for whatever comes next. It's powerful because it speaks to a deeper truth we all feel—that preparation is not just about what we do, but who we are becoming in the process. The gear-up montage is not just a preparation for survival; it's a preparation for greatness.

Let's take a moment to reflect on the story of the Exodus, specifically the night before the Hebrews left Egypt. This was not just about packing bags and readying livestock—it was about preparing for a transformational journey, a journey from slavery to freedom. The instructions given to them were meticulous: they were to eat the Passover meal in haste, with their cloaks tucked into their belts, sandals on their feet, and staff in hand. But why? Why such specific preparations?

These instructions were not merely practical necessities. They were symbolic, a physical manifestation of readiness and urgency. This was about more than escaping physical bondage; it was about embracing a mindset of freedom, a readiness to step into a new identity, to journey towards a promised future. The Hebrews were gearing up, not with weapons, but with the symbols of readiness and commitment to a cause greater than themselves.

Imagine how powerful that moment was—dressed, prepared, eating together with their families, they were not just preparing to leave; they were preparing to change. Each element of their gear-up was a reminder of their 'why'—their reason for enduring, for hoping, and for taking bold steps forward. It was about aligning their actions with their beliefs, their future, their mission.

In essence, this preparation was a declaration. It was a declaration that despite years of oppression, their spirits were unbroken, and they were ready to seize the freedom promised to them. It's a profound lesson on how our preparations reflect our intentions and our determination to pursue what we believe in, no matter the odds.

You say that you're ready for restoration, but what does your gear-up montage look like? Keep in mind the agreement between Luke 9 and Psalm 23[25]. Applying those verses here, you can receive the message: "gear-up with God's word." Get into scripture and study it in the context of your calling. Learning His nature will help you discern His voice and avoid chasing fruitless distractions.

A Crucial Step Before You Head Out

It's so common to head out on a new trek, super excited about the adventure that awaits and the spoils you'll reap. You drop the top on that convertible and see where the

---

[25] Luke 9:3 and Psalm 23:4

road takes you. It sounds so romantic, but if you do not know your "Why" it'll be tough to muster the endurance to reach your Vision.

"Why" is far more powerful than desire. Your "Why" is the core belief or purpose that inspires you to do what you do, while your "Vision" represents the future state you aspire to achieve, based on that core belief. The interplay between these two is a fundamental relationship where your "Why" acts as the foundation and driving force, and your "Vision" is the tangible manifestation of that purpose.

Foundation and Direction: Your "Why" provides the foundational reason for your actions and decisions. It's the underlying motivation for your existence, whether as an individual or an organization. The "Vision," on the other hand, is where you aim to go, guided by your "Why." It's what you strive to create or achieve as a result of your foundational beliefs.

Inspiration and Aspiration: Your "Why" is inherently inspirational; it's what gets you up in the morning and what keeps you motivated in the face of challenges. Your "Vision" is aspirational; it's a clear and compelling picture of the future that you want to create, which inspires others to join or support you in your journey.

Consistency and Adaptability: While your "Why" remains consistent and unchanging, your "Vision" can adapt based on circumstances, opportunities, and learning along the way. However, any changes in the Vision still need to align with the core "Why" to ensure that your purpose is not diluted.

Where's your bandana?

Internal and External: The "Why" is often an internal compass, shaping decisions and behaviors from within. The "Vision," while influenced internally, is expressed externally. It communicates to others what you aim to achieve and serves as a rallying call for collective action.

Feedback Loop: There is a feedback loop between your "Why" and your "Vision." Achieving milestones towards your Vision can reinforce and even deepen your understanding of your "Why," providing further clarity and conviction as you continue your pursuits.

A clear understanding of your "Why" is crucial because it ensures that your "Vision" is not just a desire or arbitrary goal but a true expression of your deepest beliefs and purposes. This alignment between "Why" and "Vision" gives you stability on the treacherous climb ahead of you.

Where's your bandana?

If your quest is a response to being called by God, then of course you must make godly decisions along the way. A man or woman of God is a person of integrity, and will not sacrifice godly values for an anticipated end. For the devout Christian, the ends never justifies the means; the means validate the end. Similarly, your Vision encapsulates your character and values. Decisions along the way may not be a matter of right or wrong, of good or evil, but one decision will often align much better with your Vision than another. It's not that the less supportive choice is wrong, it just isn't the path for you.

Even if you're not growing a business, write out a Vision of where you aspire to be. Here are some key considerations as you write it out:

> **Future Orientation:** Your Vision should describe an aspirational future state. It conveys a clear idea

of what you aim to achieve or become as a result of completing your quest.

Inspiration: It should be motivational to you. Going back and reading this during tough times should get you pumped up to stand up and get underway again.

Clarity: Keep in mind you're writing this in the context of your own excitement. Write with enough clarity that you don't need your right-now self to explain it to your future self. Consider sharing your Vision with an accountability partner (perhaps your mentor) who will also help you stay on track if you choose to diverge from your Vision later.

Brevity: Imagine needing a boost of inspiration in a moment. Something under 120 words could be printed onto a card that you keep in your pocket.

Alignment: Your Vision must align with your core values and your "Why."

Uniqueness: Your Vision cannot be cut-and-pasted; it has to come from within. Your Vision is uniquely you.

Feasibility: While a vision statement should be ambitious, it also needs to be achievable.

Integrity/Stability: Your Vision should be designed to last. You should not have to alter it because of changes of climate or seasons in your life.

These elements help ensure that your Vision effectively guides you towards a future that is both desirable and attainable, and that you honor your "Why" with every decision.

Chapter 9: The Adversary's Counterplan

"And let us not grow weary while doing good, for in due season we shall reap if we do not lose heart."

- Galatians 6:9

As believers, we are often reminded of God's grand design for our lives. However, equally crucial to understand is the adversary's counterplan, a strategy aimed at derailing us from God's path. Just as the Lord's Prayer guides us to seek divine direction, the enemy cunningly exploits our inherent weaknesses, primarily through our desires.

Imagine your desires as a double agent, pledging loyalty to you while secretly serving the enemy's interests. This covert operation begins subtly, whispering that your deepest wants are harmless or even beneficial. Yet, these desires can lead you astray, pulling you away from God.

In the Book of James[26], we learn that while we cannot control our desires, we can govern our actions in response to them. Our spiritual journey involves a constant battle between faith and flesh, a struggle vividly depicted in Galatians[27]. Here, temptation emerges as a potent weapon of war, wielded by the enemy to manipulate our desires.

The adversary's most effective tactic is not to force us into wrongdoing but to entice us to act on our own will, opposing God. This is the essence of pride—the same sin that led to Lucifer's downfall. Consumed by his splendor, Lucifer sought to usurp God's authority, resulting in his

---

[26] James 1:12
[27] Galatians 5:16-17

expulsion from heaven[28]. This narrative mirrors our struggles; the enemy aims to separate us from God by appealing to our pride and self-sufficiency. The enemy sees the temptation of self-reliance as the linchpin that separated him from God. So effective in his fall, he looks to apply the same tactic in your life to separate you from God.

Consider Eve in the Garden of Eden[29]. Tempted by the serpent, she chose to determine right and wrong independently of God. We repeat this act daily when we assess others or guide ourselves based on personal judgment rather than divine wisdom. Proverbs[30] reminds us that our hearts, the source of our desires, must align with God's word to avoid straying. That day in the

---

[28] Ezekiel 28:15-17, Isaiah 14:13-14
[29] Genesis 3:4-6
[30] Proverbs 16:23, Proverbs 4:23

garden, the serpent got under Eve's skin, into her feelings, and enticed her to see "that the tree was good for food, that it was pleasant to the eyes, and a tree desirable to make one wise". Feelings drive desires, which in turn drive actions. To counteract the adversary's plan, we must insert the influence of God's Word into this pattern. Remembering what He told us, helps us to recalibrate our desires, aligning them with God's will.

The adversary's agenda is clear: to separate us from God by using our desires against us. By recognizing this, we arm ourselves against temptation in the same manner that Christ exemplified in Luke 4. Christ's time in the wilderness serves as a masterclass in resisting the enemy's ploys. Jesus faced three primary temptations:

Self-Sufficiency: The enemy tempted Jesus to turn stones into bread, urging Him to rely on His power rather than God's provision. Jesus countered with scripture, reaffirming His dependence on God[31].

Authority and Glory: The enemy offered all the kingdoms of the world, tempting Jesus to seize power and glory for Himself. Jesus responded by worshiping God alone, rejecting self-glorification[32].

Testing God: The enemy twisted scripture to entice Jesus to test God's protection. Jesus stood firm, refusing to manipulate God's promises for personal gain[33].

---

[31] Luke 4:3-4
[32] Luke 4:5-8
[33] Luke 4:9-12

Understand the Adversary's Counterplan

Through these responses, Jesus demonstrated the importance of knowing God's nature and adhering to His word. Our defense against temptation lies in this same principle: grounding ourselves in scripture to discern and resist the enemy's tactics.

What do you want?

Temptation is an ongoing battle. The adversary's true cunning lies in tempting you to act on what you perceive as right, often turning your own desires into tools of rebellion. By understanding this strategy, you can better defend yourself, ensuring your actions reflect God's will rather than your flawed human judgment. This is highly relevant on your road to restoration. Of course, you're on this road because you desire to be higher in station, to be restored or to be elevated. When your desire becomes greater than your sense of righteousness, you can separate yourself from the One Who called you. Worse, you can disqualify yourself from the promised land you're striving to reach.

What do you want?

Remember, it's not only inherently wicked desires that lead us astray but also the misuse of our desires, even the neutral or good ones. The adversary's ultimate goal is to tempt you to govern yourself, using your desires against you. Stay vigilant, immerse yourself in God's Word enough to understand His nature, and let His guidance lead you through the perils of temptation.

Chapter 10: The Perilous Journey

You've seen or at least heard of those epic cinematic quests where the hero treks for weeks, months, or at least a scene or two before reaching the castle or innermost cave where the treasure awaits. Along the way, there's a challenge, a treacherous road to travel, or worse... an agent sent by the enemy to discourage our hero and send him back from whence he came. We see this played out so often because it's a perfect framework in which to create the hero's character arc. A character arc is a transformation or inner journey of a character over the course of a story. The character begins as one sort of person and transforms into a different sort of person in response to changing developments in the story. The events along the way build strength and confidence and test resilience and faith.

The Perilous Journey

Although the *5 Steps to Find True Love* took five weeks to receive, study, and fully understand, the process can be much quicker than that. By Christmas, I was fully prepared, right down to tying on my bandana, and I was ready to earnestly seek my bride. I had to make one minor pitstop first. Although my eyesight had been superb my entire life, my age was starting to show. I went in to see an ophthalmologist for eyeglasses and came out with a brain tumor! A meningioma is a tumor that forms on the layers of membranes that cover the brain. They are very slow-growing, and most commonly benign. They are so innocuous that it's common practice to leave them alone, taking no action until it causes a problem. In my case, it was growing on my optic nerve and thus affecting my eyesight. The irony is not lost on me; while I was growing progressively blind spiritually, I was also growing progressively blind physically.

The Perilous Journey

At first, no worries, many said it would be an endoscopic procedure, maybe even outpatient. But when the doctor described the required bifrontal craniotomy, I could not stop crying out of fear... and a sense of worthlessness. I never thought I would be alone in a moment like this. The spiritual challenge had begun.

The surgery was a success! Vision restored, though I am now committed to wearing eyeglasses. However, the real peril was just beginning as the inner voice of demons grew louder. They reminded me how worthless I was for not having a wife to help me through this. The voices were in the mirror as I saw how the visible trauma and staples made me feel like a monster. "You thought you were about to find your bride, but who's going to want you now?!" Worse, I was taking the prescribed anti-seizure medication which caused severe depression.

The Perilous Journey

When friends visited, I silently looked forward to returning to my solitude. An empty house, filled only with my destructive thoughts, allowed me to wrap myself in that depression like a warm blanket on a winter's night.

In the depth of my emotions, the physical trauma felt like a grotesque mask I could not take off, and the emotional pain was an insidious whisper, always reminding me of my isolation and perceived worthlessness. Each day was a struggle to muster the will to get out of bed, to face a world that seemed to mirror my internal desolation. My house, once a place of solitude, had become a cavern of despair where shadows of doubt and fear danced around me, mocking my every effort to rise above my circumstances.

The Perilous Journey

I saw my reflection and recoiled, not just from the visible scars but from the metaphorical ones that had been ripped open by this ordeal. My depression was like an oppressive fog, thick and suffocating, wrapping itself around me and making every step feel like I was wading through quicksand. The medications, meant to heal, instead seemed to deepen my descent into this abyss, each pill a bitter reminder of my fragility and failure.

The inner voice of demons, ever-present, whispered lies of inadequacy and doom, "You're alone in this. No one will ever love you again." The weight of their words pressed down on my chest, making it hard to breathe, let alone hope. They preyed on my deepest fears and insecurities, exploiting my moments of weakness to magnify my self-doubt and sorrow.

The Perilous Journey

It was in this crucible of despair that I clung to the preparation and promises of God's Word. The *5 **Steps to Find True Love*** were not just a guide but a lifeline, anchoring me to the truth when all around me felt like shifting sand. After the staples were removed, the swelling subsided, and signs of surgical trauma had faded from the natural eye of passers-by, I decided to step into the dating world again. With my shattered self-image, this was a tremendous step into the unknown, a defiant act against the darkness that had recently consumed me.

In retrospect, I see that these voices were the agents of the enemy, sent to deter me, distract me, and discourage me from continuing on my quest. They nearly won because I started to pursue casual dates just to see if I was even remotely desirable, or perhaps to prove those inner voices right. I was shocked! It did not take too many coffeeshop meet-ups to realize that women were not rejecting me. Just the opposite. Part of my gear-up was the *5 Steps*, and they kept me from settling for simple validation. I was still on mission to find my bride. Technically, I never did find her; rather, she found me. A simple "Hello" on the dating app from some girl who called herself "Beautiful44." There were so many red flags, but I'm pretty good at spotting fake profiles. She claimed to be just two years younger than me, but her picture looked half my age. Still, her write-up spoke to me like a kindred spirit in His Kingdom. We decided to meet.

In meeting her, I was not just stepping into the innermost cave of my quest; I was stepping into a new understanding of God's grace and timing. This perilous journey, marked by trials and tribulations, had brought me to the brink of giving up, only to reveal the depths of my resilience and faith. It was in the darkest moments that I found the light of His presence, guiding me towards the promised land He had prepared for me.

Understanding Your Adversity

In human warfare, adversaries follow a standard principle: eliminate the threat. We should expect the same strategy in spiritual warfare. In the faith, some say to their friends who are going through struggles, "there must be a great calling on your life." While that's comforting to hear when you're the one going through adversity, it's better to consider all the possible reasons why things are rough for you on your path of ascension:

1. You're doing the right thing. The enemy is attacking you to eliminate a threat. This is the one you want to believe because it gives you a greater sense of God being on your side. But, is it always true? A great way to determine is to revisit your "Why." Why are you on this quest? Why do you feel you've been called? Or better yet, why do you wish to get to your goal? What will you do when you get there? If your journey and destination will advance the Kingdom, the enemy will want to deter you.

2. You're on the right quest, but not on the right path.

This situation is really quite common because it is born of excitement. You were called and plunged headlong into your mission. You have your own ideas of how to get this done, but did you pray and meditate on them, seeking guidance from the Holy Spirit?

Consider Paul and his companions, which included Silas and likely Timothy, traveling through the region of Phrygia and Galatia. They had intended to preach the gospel in the province of Asia, which at the time was a region in the western part of modern Turkey. However, the Holy Spirit did not allow them to enter the area. The scripture does not detail the exact means through which the Spirit prevented their plans, but it's clear that their path was decisively redirected, and that Paul was obedient to His ongoing guidance.

As they reached the border of Mysia, they tried to enter Bithynia, a region to the north, but again the Spirit of Jesus did not permit them to do so. As a result, they went down to Troas, a city on the Aegean coast. It was here that Paul had a vision in the night: a man from Macedonia stood and pleaded with him, saying, "Come over to Macedonia and help us." After Paul had the vision, they immediately sought to go to Macedonia, concluding that God had called them to preach the gospel there instead.

3. You misinterpreted your call (or weren't called to begin with). You're not a threat to the enemy, just a victim of your own foolishness. If you accept foolishness to be the opposite of wisdom, and wisdom to begin with the fear of God and following His precepts, you can accept 'going rogue' in your ascent to be a matter of foolishness.

So, when the going gets tough, it could be that you're 1) being attacked, 2) being corrected, or 3) trying to make your own way. In a secular context, you could add other options like karma, coincidence, and good old-fashioned bad luck. However, if you believe in your calling and you believe in God's plan, these notions do not have a place for consideration. Bottom line, revisit your reasons for this journey and the path you're taking through the lens of God's Word.

Chapter 11: The Innermost Cave

In those epic tales, when the hero finally reaches the castle or cave of treasures, there is always a sense of caution. The wise adventurer is wary because the treasure, sitting in plain view, just cannot be that easy to claim, right? Booby traps, trap doors, secret codes, or tricks of illusion often protect the real treasure. These obstacles are not there to make the treasure impossible to reach, but rather to ensure that only the worthy can claim the prize.

I had to proceed cautiously with this "Beautiful" girl. Was this treasure truly what she seemed, and was this the treasure God set aside for me? Was this where I was supposed to be, or merely where I wanted to be? The inquisition began:

What's your real name? "Lynne"

The Innermost Cave

What's your favorite color? "Blue"

Who's the most important person in your life? "I have three most-important persons: the Father, the Son, and the Holy Spirit, because I'm a Proverbs 31 woman."

She got spiritual and sassy with me in the same sentence! Ok, let's see how this plays out!

Turns out, Lynne had walked through a tough time herself, leaning on her faith to pull her through. Her ex-husband had suddenly up and left her for another woman, and her heart was left in ruins. She hit her own rock bottom and did a lot of work on herself to put the trauma of betrayal behind her. Eventually, she put herself out there and spent a short time on dating apps. A short time was all she needed to realize how debaucherous guys can be. Deciding to send one more message before giving up, she got on her face, then got online, and saw my profile. After a moment of "Wow, God, you work fast!" she sent that "Hello." Unbeknownst to her, it was my birthday. At first glance, she seemed too good to be true. Like that treasure in plain sight, I was wary of trap doors and booby traps. But with what God had shown me in the *5 Steps*, I quickly determined that she was the real deal, genuine, authentic, pure gold.

I knew I had to treat her right to be worthy of the prize, but I still had crabs undercover in my life. When hearing of my commitment to purity until marriage with her, another friend of mine, a pastor and ministry leader, spoke out in disbelief: "There's no way, there's no way you're going to hold off until marriage. Man, don't fool yourself. You know you're going to be sleeping together in a few weeks." He kept saying, "There's no way!" I should have responded with, "Get behind me, satan." But I just quietly let him think whatever; I knew our commitment to God was solid. Even without booby traps, that may have been my first test. Just like my friend had the voice of the enemy, Lynne had the voice of an angel. That voice rose up on our third date.

I had always gauged how well a date went by whether or not it ended with a kiss. On that first date with Lynne, I got a little worried when she was a little late. She arrived, beautiful as ever, having spent hours to look just right, but for me, really, I was just happy she showed up! We might have shut the sushi place down that night; conversation with her was so interesting, so engaging. I typically coach people to leave some mystery to uncover in subsequent dates, but with Lynne, I felt like I could share everything with her in an instant, and there would still be more to discover with her the next day. We stepped outside, said our goodbyes, and called it a night. I was so content with our time together that I did not need the superficial validation of a kiss. We would see each other again, soon.

The second date almost did not happen because it was her birthday, and she was super busy running errands. She paused for a moment for me to catch up with her and give her a bouquet and a card with a symbolic mustard seed. She cherished the biblical reference but had to get moving. Rushed, it just did not feel like the right time for our first kiss.

Third date, this was it! She selected the beautiful Japanese Tea Gardens with its flora, waterfalls, and koi fish setting the mood. "This is it!" I thought. I was so excited on the inside, I had to work to keep it cool on the outside. Then she stopped in front of the main waterfall, and I could see

myself like a cartoon character... eyes closed, leaning

forward with my lips puckered six inches out from my

face! But instead of that kiss, I received the words, "Rob,

we have to go slow." Wait, what? "I haven't even kissed

you yet," I thought. "How much slower can we go?!"

Instead of saying that, though, I simply agreed that I was

looking for something lasting and getting to know each

other was key. I truly believed that, but I sure did want to

kiss her!!! We'll call this patience, because it would be

melodramatic to call it longsuffering.

In past relationships, I would be the one to fall in love

fast, then get my heart ripped out. Mara had me

questioning what love even is. I never had that in-love

feeling with her, but I thought the act of loving someone

would be enough. Not so much. With Lynne, for objective

and intangible reasons, I loved her... truly. But I refused to get caught in the Chemistry Trap again, the trap of falling in love with the feeling of being in love without having a truly reciprocal love relationship. In other words, I had decided that she would say those three words first. I had it all planned out. One day we would embrace, she would gaze into my eyes and say, "I love you, Rob." And I would return a warm smile and say, "I knew I loved you before I met you." OK, who cares that those were lyrics from a Savage Garden song; it was perfect! Except, she had also made the same decision to not say those words first. Stalemate! Neither of us was willing to take that leap of faith.

That Holy Spirit though, His Spirit did His work on me! It's like He had a side-conversation with me during yet another impactful sermon. He pointed out, Rob, that girl's heart is not just your treasure, her heart is your promised land, but there's a fortress around her heart. You cannot bust through or tear it down. You'll have to speak to her the way I tell you to, and I'm telling you to tell her how you feel. Oh, Lord, really?! Talk about facing your greatest fears on the trail of tribulations. I'm all about intentional obedience. So, I guess it's time.

My problem was that, despite my love for her, I was not fully committed to her yet. I kept looking for signs from her that she was committed to me before I gave her my heart. Even the words she used to describe our relationship were a concern to me. She would tell people that I was 'a guy she's talking to'. Week after week I'd ask if I could call her my girlfriend, and she would always respond, "Not yet." I wanted to give my all to her, but not if she was holding back! But this sermon moved me, it pushed me, it made me reevaluate how I worship my God. It made me see that I had to change my ways to practice my faith. If I truly believed He brought me through the wilderness, to this place in time, to this promised land, then how could I not believe in Him now?

For our next date I went all in. I cooked her an amazing dinner, flowers and candlelight, and of course we enjoyed a robust, engaging conversation. Dinner was perfect (which is a miracle in itself), and dessert was divine! When we stood up from the table, I spoke my heart, and whatever I said included the words, "I love you." The kiss that followed was fireworks over the moon... the kiss of ages... a moment I could have frozen and lived in forever. She did not reciprocate the words, but she did not have to. As we loosened our embrace, she stepped back and declared she had to go. She gathered her things so quickly that I feared I had done something terribly wrong. I walked her to her car, and our final kiss reassured me, no, nothing is wrong, nothing at all. The walls around her heart had come tumbling down.

As a general practice, we kept our dates in public, until we did not. After that kiss, that angel voice came back saying, "Rob, promise me that if I come over we will not cross any lines." She would say that before every date, and each time I would promise. So, then, I had to realize, I could not even try to get too intimate because I would clearly be breaking a promise to her if I did, and she would be the first witness of my betrayal. How could she ever trust me when we're apart if I cannot honor her wishes when we're together? So, we ended up honoring our Father's plan for the covenant. I was in! And it was only by honoring Him and following His plan.

Search Your Heart

Booby traps and trap doors are often replaced with tests of faith in Kingdom quests. This is not to say you'll never be led into temptation, but your faith in Christ can deliver you from evil if you transfer your trust to Him. This is life: forks in the road, your angels and your demons at war. In this maze of mirrors, your cold desire turns your sense of honor into a brittle shield. Yet, when you awaken to His Light and feel comforted by His presence, you instinctively know the right path. That path is clear if you have a clear focus on Christ.

Your test of faith may not even seem like a test at all. We think of tests as decisions to make. Placed in a given situation, which path do you take? Job's tests of faith were more about his reactions than his decisions. He deeply laments his misfortune and questions why he, a righteous man, must suffer so grievously. He curses the day of his birth[34] and expresses a wish to die, highlighting the depth of his despair.

The conversations and monologues of Job about his suffering primarily occur from Chapters 3 to 31. In these verses, Job's friends—Eliphaz, Bildad, and Zophar—offer traditional perspectives that suffering is a consequence of sin and argue that Job must have committed offenses that he must confess. They assert that God is just and that Job's suffering must be a divine punishment. As his friends repeatedly insist that his suffering must be due to some hidden sin, Job becomes increasingly frustrated. He describes his pain and misery in vivid detail and laments

---

[34] Job 3:1

the absence of justice in his situation. His speeches convey a profound sense of isolation and misunderstanding.

Through this turmoil, Job expresses a desire for God to reveal any hidden sins or faults in him that might have caused his suffering: "How many are my iniquities and sins? Make me know my transgression and my sin."[35] This reflects Job's perplexity and his quest for understanding regarding his suffering, as he maintains his innocence yet remains open to being corrected if he is indeed in the wrong.

In Chapter 31, Job goes through a detailed self-examination, listing possible sins and declaring his innocence in each case. He invites God to weigh him on

---

[35] Job 13:23

honest scales and to account for any wrongdoing[36]. This chapter is essentially Job's final plea for justice and a clear conscience before God, illustrating his continued effort to understand his suffering within the framework of his belief in divine justice and his own integrity.

God responds to Job starting from Chapter 38 by challenging him, but the tone and content of God's response can be interpreted as both admonishing and enlightening. God speaks from a whirlwind and begins by questioning Job, which serves to underscore the vast gap in knowledge and power between God and man. God's speech addresses not only Job's questioning of divine justice but also corrects the presumptions by Job and his friends about how the world works and how God administers justice. It serves to remind Job of his place in

---

[36] Job 31:6

the grand scheme of things and to reorient his perspective from the myopic view of his personal suffering to the broader context of God's governance over the whole universe. God does not directly answer Job's questions about why the righteous suffer. Instead, God focuses on His sovereignty and the wisdom inherent in His management of the world. This approach shifts the discussion from a debate over justice to an acknowledgment of divine authority and mystery.

How often have you stood before God and proclaimed, "I don't deserve this." I have, and my pastor was rather quick to correct me. "By whose measure are you undeserving of struggle and strife? Do you really want to get what you truly deserve?"

You may face calamity when you seem to have it all within reach, and you may be tempted to try to make sense of it. I encourage you to not focus on why you're facing difficulties in the 11th-hour, but rather:

1. Check your ego. Avoid slipping into Job-level lamentation because, ultimately, he did nothing but expose his inability to understand God's plan.

2. Reassess your heart. Check your motivations and honestly discern if you want to reach your goal to satisfy self or to glorify God.

3. Focus on your "Why." Why do you want to reach that goal, and what is your Vision of life when you get there? If designed properly and you have faith in the calling upon your life, your Why and Vision will propel you through any adversity.

Chapter 12: The Point of Surrender

Understanding yourself is a crucial part of knowing when you have reached your limits. People often say, "At the end of you is the beginning of God," but that's an oversimplification. "In the beginning was the Word, and the Word was with God, and the Word was God...." There is no beginning of God that we can comprehend, but we can recognize when it's time to let go because there's nothing more we can do. This moment of realization is typically when someone surrenders to His will.

I prided myself on knowing myself well. I understood that my romantic relationships often hit a turning point after a specific period. Consistently throughout my life, dynamics and feelings shifted after a certain number of months. I advised myself against making any long-term decisions during that time, but rather use that time to gain assurance about who we truly are as individuals together, and as a couple. So I went back to Pastor Ethan, the man who insisted that Mara had to leave my life for me to heal. He and his wife conducted relationship assessments, and they concluded that I was much healthier, and that I had found a real gem in Lynne. However, he warned us about seeing things through rose-colored glasses. We were still in the new-relationship energy phase where it seems nothing could ever go wrong. Our relationship had not yet reached the turning point where I could see the true Lynne. I knew that, so I waited. Even when she started asking about when I was going to pop the question, I told her I had to meet her folks first. Her dad was out of the picture, so I at least needed to get her mom's blessing.

Another test. We drove from San Antonio, TX to Rock Island, IL—a 34-hour round trip for a weekend—just to ask her mom for her blessing to pursue Lynne for marriage. When I asked, she nearly jumped out of her chair. "Praise God! Praise God!!!" she started cheering in the middle of the restaurant. Then she grabbed her phone saying, "I gotta tell everyone!" "Whoa... whoa, whoa, whoa..." I had to reel her back. "I have not asked her to marry me yet. I was asking for your blessing before I do!" This was just one indication that our courtship was indeed the best of times. Lynne was my best friend and confidante. I could tell her anything, and I told her everything. Yet and still, there was one more major test remaining for us, for me.

On the day of our engagement, we headed back to the Japanese Tea Gardens where we almost had our first kiss.

The Point of Surrender

I had planned to head right back to that waterfall, drop to a knee, and sing my proposal to her. Instead, the Gardens were bustling with costumed kids; it was Halloween weekend! So, we returned to the actual spot of our first kiss and I carried out my plan. On one knee, singing completed, ring presented, her first reaction was to laugh! That's classic for us; we're always finding joy in simple moments. Not malicious, it was an innocent nervous laughter that made the moment perfect. Yes, she said yes, and we immediately set a date nestled in between our April birthdays. I had taken one more major step toward the prize of wedded bliss with a godly woman; I had just a few short months to go!

I felt blessed and in control, which is actually somewhat of an oxymoron. When you try to control things you can disqualify yourself from God's blessings. I had managed our courtship well, and she was brimming with the excitement of becoming my wife for the rest of our lives. But within a month of engagement, the demons of my past caught up with me. The mountain of marital and business debts came crashing down on me. An onslaught of notices came in waves in the mail, some of them threatening to garnish my wages that were already just barely enough to support us. For a moment, I stressed. Seriously, who faces this right after getting engaged, and remains engaged? I imagine many women would have insisted that I get all that mess sorted out before any wedding could happen, but that was not Lynne's heart.

Honesty and transparency have been cornerstones of our relationship from the start. Before we met I had taken part in various activities that were not becoming of a Christ-follower and I did not withhold any of that from

Lynne. She had never been one to judge or condemn; that's just part of her beauty. But this was different. My past was exactly that, my past. It painted a picture of a person I used to be and heart I used to have, but she had faith that God had given me a new heart and put a new spirit in me[37]. She could witness the fruit of His Spirit in my daily living. But this news... this was far more real than ancient history. This news would shape her future in a way that most people would veer away from. That old me may have tried to cover this up and attempt to control a situation that was already out of control. I had to surrender; I had to let go and let God do His work. Jokes and laughing aside, I got real and disclosed the direness of the situation to Lynne.

---

[37] Ezekiel 36:26

The Point of Surrender

She did not flinch, back down, or turn away. She very calmly suggested filing Chapter 7. I had always considered bankruptcy to be for losers. Before I told her, I feared that filing would scare her away. But she suggested it. She supported it. She saw my future as our future, regardless of the strains and stresses. Following through with this would affect where we live and how we live for the next seven years, but she was more than okay with that. She was truly my partner, through thick and thin. My fear turned into a celebration because we could start our life together without being encumbered by my past. This sequence of events forced me to face my greatest fear of losing all that I had gained on my path of restoration. I had tried to do everything right, down to telling Lynne about my unsavory past relationships. Turns out, all that previous disclosure spoke to my character and established that my oversights were not intentional deceptions.

Your Leap of Faith

Glory is right there, almost within reach! Your holy grail is near but there's one last test. A cinematic parallel to your predicament is the end of *Indiana Jones and the Last Crusade*. Indy faces three trials in the final steps to reach the Holy Grail. His first clue, "Only the penitent man will pass," indicated that he must show humility and kneel before God. The second trial had him acknowledge Who he was surrendering to (stepping on stones that spelled out the name of God), and the third trial was a leap of faith.

In Matthew 14[38], we see Peter taking a bold step of faith. He steps out of the boat and walks on water toward Jesus. This moment may provide some key insight for the final steps of your quest.

And Peter answered Him and said, "Lord, if it is You, command me to come to You on the water." So He said, "Come." And when Peter had come down out of the boat, he walked on the water to go to Jesus. But when he saw that the wind was boisterous, he was afraid; and

[38] Matthew 14:28-31

beginning to sink he cried out, saying, "Lord, save me!" And immediately Jesus stretched out His hand and caught him, and said to him, "O you of little faith, why did you doubt?"

What will be your critical moment, and how will you handle it? What will be your reason for taking your leap of faith?

- **Naïveté:** You may not realize the danger and you just do it.

  Sometimes, stepping out in faith feels safe because we don't fully grasp the risks involved. Like Peter, who did not calculate the wind and waves, our innocence can propel us to move forward. In these moments, our lack of awareness could potentially be foolishness, yes, but it could also be a profound opportunity to witness God's power in our weakness. When we do not see the full scope of danger, we might just see the full scope of God's potential to save us.

For you, this is a reminder to keep your eyes on the One Who called you, even when unanticipated dangerous distractions are pulling your focus away. Discerning His voice from the beginning of this journey was encouraged for times like this, so that you would know Who you're putting your faith in when you take that leap of faith. It's okay to not know everything that could blind-side you, as long as you remain focused on what He would have you do.

- **Fatigue:** The journey has made you weary and numb, and you just want to get it over with.

Your Leap of Faith

There are times when the grind of life leaves us exhausted, and we leap simply because we cannot bear to stay where we are. Peter, fatigued by fear and the struggle against the storm, may have stepped out in a moment of weary surrender. In our fatigue, we find a raw and real encounter with God, where our strength ends and we more deeply recognize His presence. It's in our weariness that His invitation to "Come" is most compelling, promising rest and renewal.

Fatigue is a tough one. In Peter's case, he may have leapt to reach respite, but what if you are simply so weary that you have no faith in the leap? You do it only because you're supposed to or because it's the next step. If faith without works is dead, then works without faith is just activity. You simply cannot walk out God's plan without faith. When faced with a leap of faith, be very conscious and intentional about placing that faith in Him. Carry that divine faith through storms and winds, carry it all the way to your goal. And if the leap does not align with His nature, He is not the one who's calling you. Discern His voice.

- **Excitement: You got this far... let's go!**
Faith also springs from a place of exhilaration. Peter's heart raced with the possibility of walking towards Jesus on the water. That same thrill can ignite your faith journey, pushing you beyond the familiar and into the extraordinary. A leap triggered by excitement is not necessarily reckless. If it's an authentic divine enthusiasm, a joy in seeing just how far God can take you. Then your

excitement reflects divine trust. When our hearts are on fire with holy excitement, we leap, ready to see what God will do next. However, if your excitement is blinding you such that you cannot see anything, including Christ, stand down! Calm down and ask, "Lord, if it is You, command me to come to You." Find your quiet place, pray, and meditate on His Word. You may need to be intentionally discerning in your excitement.

- **Desperation:** You realize that you've done all you can do on your own, or you have lost faith in yourself.

Desperation may sound like a negative, inadvisable reason to leap, but it can be a powerful catalyst for faith. When you reach the end of your abilities, resources, and self-reliance, you're left with one option: to cry out to Jesus. Peter's sinking moment is a vivid reminder that our desperation can drive us to the Savior. It's in these Hail Mary moments, these final throes of faith, that we experience the most profound rescues. When our faith falters, Jesus' hand is already reaching out, ready to catch us.

It's at the point of desperation that you stop relying on self. One of our biggest flaws is the "I got this!" mentality. You shout it as a battle cry and even relish in your peers encouraging you with the sentiment. But if you always "got this," then why would you need faith in Christ? Why would you need His covering or protection? Why would you even need His call? Just call yourself! But those who follow Him will hand their reins over to Him and go where He leads, even when He calls you to make a leap of faith.

In each of these scenarios, whether it's naïveté, fatigue, excitement, or desperation, the common thread is the presence of Jesus and His unwavering faithfulness. Your reasons for stepping out in faith might differ, but His response remains constant: He is there, ready to lift us, guide us, and grow your faith. So, discern His voice and surrender to Him in these crucial steps toward restoration.

Chapter 13: The Promised Land

A kiss at the altar. Rice and bouquet in the air. Closing papers signed and keys to your new home. Ribbon-cutting, open for business. Diploma in hand, tassel turned. Remission Day, you're cancer-free! Gripping your 1-year Chip. You made it! Whether a sprint or a marathon, you've crossed the finish line! Like reaching the beach, you just want to bask in the warmth of your victory. But how long does that last, really? You get back from the honeymoon, graduation celebrations end, you walk through the front door of your new home. What now? Do you go back to your normal life? I submit to you that if your journey was transformational, the normal you knew does not (or at least should not) exist anymore.

The Old You:

You were called from that place. Like moving out of an old house into the new, you would not go back to live in that old house. Right?

The Recent You:

Spiritually, mentally, maybe even physically you've been on the road trying to get to this place. You would not go back to sleep on the bus after your arrival. Right?

For me, married life was both familiar and new. My first marriage was hedonistic, meaning that it was focused more on pleasure and self-indulgence than the values that God calls us to honor. Although hedonism often carries the connotation of debauchery, that is not what I mean here. For example, marrying because of the way he cooks, or the way she makes you feel, or the house, cars, and lavish lifestyle... these are all examples of pleasure, self-indulgence... hedonism. Now, of course, yes, I truly enjoyed (and I still enjoy) how Lynne makes me feel. We've got great chemistry, but she made it clear from the jump, "I need you to love God more than you love me." In kind, I vowed nothing to her at our wedding. You see, while many grooms offer love, respect, patience, and faithfulness, I promised none of these things to her. Instead, I made one vow in saying to her, "I vow surrender to God our Father in our marriage. That means my faithfulness to you is based on my faithfulness to God. My dedication to be kind, patient, honest, and forgiving comes from God's grace upon me. And even knowing what an amazing angel you are in my life, I will never question if I'm worthy of your love because God has validated and confirmed me as worthy. I am your husband in the full capacity of God's plan for marriage." After what I went through to get to that stage in my life with such an amazingly godly woman, I knew I wanted our marriage to be extraordinary. Not extraordinary by the measure of man, but rather the uncommon covenant that God designed for us all. How could I accept His leading of me to this place, and not honor Him as I occupy this place?

Despite that sincere vow, the first year of our marriage was all about us. Our honeymoon getaway was followed by the whirlwind of finding our first marital home and moving two households into it, then settling in (which seemed to last forever). Before we knew it, life was upon us and we were managing the dynamics of a new marriage while re-integrating into our work lives. It was all about us.

Sure, there was a lot of enjoyment and contentment. But before too long we realized that was not enough. No, this was not a materialistic hunger, it was a realization that we were not gifted this marriage to only honor God, we were here to also worship Him through this marital team-up. Honoring God and worshipping God through our works are two beautiful yet distinct ways we live out our faith, each with its own unique expression of devotion.

Honoring God:

This is about reflecting His character in everything we do. It's about living a life that mirrors His love, grace, and truth in our daily interactions. When we honor God, we're showcasing His presence in our lives through our actions and decisions. It's about integrity, kindness, and obedience to His Word. Think of it as the day-to-day testimony of our faith, the quiet yet powerful witness that others see in how we conduct ourselves. Honoring God means we make choices that align with His teachings, and we seek to bring glory to His name through our conduct, whether at work, at home, or in our communities.

Worshipping God through Our Works:

This takes it a step further. Worship is about ascribing worth and reverence to God, acknowledging His supreme value in our lives. When we worship God through our works, we're not just acting rightly out of duty or moral obligation; we're offering our actions as a form of praise. It's about dedicating our efforts, our talents, and our labor as acts of worship. Imagine every task you undertake, no matter how mundane, being offered up as a fragrant offering to God. It's a mindset where we say, "Lord, this work is for You. May it honor and please You." Worship through works is an intentional act of love and devotion, recognizing that everything we do is an opportunity to exalt our Creator.

In essence, while honoring God is about reflecting His nature in our everyday life, worshipping God through our works is about intentionally dedicating our efforts as acts of praise and adoration. Both are vital expressions of our faith, drawing us closer to Him and allowing His light to shine through us in all we do.

We were delivered to this promised land not just to praise and thank Him, but also to serve Him, to walk it out. There was yet much work to do.

Your Arrival

Sometimes your deliverance has a clear what-to-do when your boots hit the ground. In the case of a business finally getting the green light, you execute the business plan you established as led by His Spirit. Even when your what-to-do is not obvious, conduct yourself in this stage full of honor for The One Who called you here. Sometimes reaching a milestone can bring on a feeling of uncertainty pressing on your shoulders. You know you're supposed to do something, so you get busy not realizing that your busyness can separate you from God. "Be still and know that I am God," is the instruction you may miss in trying to determine your own proceeding path. Suggesting that you wait patiently for a word from the Lord to guide your next steps does not suggest a cessation of activity. It is for you to remain mindful of His presence, nature, and Word at every step so that your God-sanctioned path to advance is clear. Consider David.

Anointed as a young shepherd boy to be the future king of Israel, David spent years waiting and often fleeing for his life from King Saul. He sought God's guidance repeatedly, like in 2 Samuel, where he asked, "Shall I go up against the Philistines? Will You deliver them into my hand?" And the Lord said to David, "Go up, for I will doubtless deliver the Philistines into your hand."[39] David's success came from his willingness to wait for God's instructions and move only when he received a clear word.

You will be busy in your new life, but will you become so busy that God's voice becomes attenuated, turning you to

---

[39] 2 Samuel 5:19

find your own way? This happens quickly and easily when your new success keeps you out of His Word, out of church, and out of fellowship with your brethren. Even if your new life is all about ministry, you can get so wrapped up in the activity of growing the mission that you lose sight of the point of the mission. This stage is crucial for you because there is likely more for you to receive if you deepen your relationship with Him. He may have led you here to get your attention, so you could hear him better. So, amidst your busyness, carve out time to get in your quiet time and listen for His proceeding word for you.

Chapter 14: Mysteries Revealed

When I started on my restoration journey, about 1½ years before I met Lynne, I felt God calling me into marriage ministry. He gave me a holistic perspective that the best way to save a marriage is by preparing the heart of the single person before they meet someone special. As I grew in this calling, the news of marriages dissolving was distressing to me. I felt the distress of each divorce in my own heart, knowing it could have been avoided. My call in this area was undeniable, and my passion for helping singles and couples only deepened over time. So firmly planted in this call, I declared to Lynne on our first date that I was heading into marriage ministry. Although saying something so bold and presumptuous so early could have easily triggered her to sprint to the exit, she responded by saying that she had been called into "a love ministry" and did not know what that meant until that moment. Clearly, that's where God wanted me to land, right? Actually, He was getting me there to speak to me in ways that I did not have the capacity to hear at the start.

Lynne and I studied together, got marriage-help certifications together, and earned advanced degrees together. You see, my initial thought of 'helping marriages' went only as far as applying Biblical concepts and precepts. That was the perfect place to start, but I was effectively a layman, an uneducated dating coach with a sincere heart to help. That's what I could see of myself, and that's all I felt called to be at the start of my mission. God guided my steps into studying human psychology, which helped me realize that each of us is made of both flesh and spirit. If you minister to only one, then you minister to only part of the person. I had to broaden my perspectives to integrate secular and Christian counseling. Of course, our degrees required a broader base of study as well: Marriage and Family Therapy, Divorce Aftercare, Crisis and Abuse Therapy, Counseling for Anger and Depression, Pre-engagement / Pre-marital Counseling, Struggles with Self-control, Inner-peace and Productivity, and the Pursuit of Peace and Restoration, all became areas of intense study.

As we established a private practice to focus on romantic relationships, God began priming me through my wife as she would say, "we need to do more than just marriages." Even though I trust my wife implicitly, I did not have the capacity to receive that word while on the journey. However, after we completed our graduate studies and I took a moment to "be still and know that He is God," I was struck with a proceeding word that raised the bar on my mission. As a result, we founded Eternal Light Christian Counseling Services as a nonprofit clinic to make Christian Counseling more accessible for individuals and families to heal, grow, and restore their peace. Through Eternal Light, we are now applying our training and experience to address a greater set of needs in the community, helping counselees experience the guiding and healing hand of Christ as applied to a broader scope of life challenges. Starting with a firm footing on His Word and His guidance, our vision goes far beyond the original calling. I had to get to where I was called so that I could receive my next assignment and elevate even higher, for Him.

Sometimes God withholds certain understandings until we are ready to receive them. This concept is not just a matter of God keeping secrets but more so about Him preparing us to handle the truths He wants to reveal. He encourages us to cull our activity at times such that we enter a headspace and heart-space where we can receive Him. The best example may be in Luke 24[40], where Jesus tells His disciples, "I am going to send you what my Father has promised; but stay in the city until you have been clothed with power from on high." (NIV) Here, Jesus is speaking about the coming of the Holy Spirit, a critical element for the disciples' mission ahead. But notice, they had to wait—they were not yet ready to step into the fullness of their calling without the empowerment of the Holy Spirit. It's not that Jesus wanted to withhold this power from them; rather, it was about them being in the right position and maturity to receive it. God had a mystery reserved for the right moment, and at Pentecost, this mystery moved

---

[40] Luke 24:49

into a revelation where their higher station of serving could begin.

Then Jesus explains, "I still have many things to say to you, but you cannot bear them now. However, when He, the Spirit of truth, has come, He will guide you into all truth; for He will not speak on His own authority, but whatever He hears He will speak; and He will tell you things to come."[41] Here Jesus explicitly acknowledges that there are things the disciples are not yet ready to handle. It's not a matter of reluctance from Jesus to share, but an understanding of the disciples' current capacity. The promise, however, is that the Spirit of Truth—when they are ready—will guide them into all truth. Again, we see the movement from mystery to revelation.

---

[41] John 16:12-13

What we glean from these passages is a comforting and exhilarating reminder: God is always in the process of unveiling His plans to us at the perfect time. The mysteries that God withholds are indeed for us—they are treasures stored up, waiting for the moment when we are equipped and mature enough to handle them. And when we are ready, these mysteries turn into revelations that we are then called to steward wisely.

In essence, God's timing is perfect, and His revelations are profound. As we grow and mature in our faith, we can trust that He will reveal more of His truth to us, equipping us to fulfill the call He has placed on our lives.

Rise up!

When you were called, you had a certain, limited capacity to receive. If you got to this promised land, clearly you had the capacity to receive part of His revelation and the will to follow. Understand, you were not restored for your own pleasure. You were not elevated for your own enjoyment. You've been given a gift to give back and help others. The trials of the journey have served to give you strength and maturity so you can receive your true calling and step into it. Your experiences and triumphs over your trials and tribulations have hopefully deepened your faith and fellowship with the Father. Certainly, you do not think it was your own strength and skill that carried you through.

Rise up!

There are three basic behaviors to carry out in this stage of your journey to receive the full revelation of God's plan for you:

1. Obedience to God,

2. Fellowship with God,

3. Graceful Acceptance.

We see all three behaviors demonstrated by the disciples in Acts 1[42]. After Jesus' ascension, the disciples returned to Jerusalem as instructed in Luke 24[43] and went up to the room where they were staying. The scripture notes that they all joined together continually in prayer, along with the women and Mary the mother of Jesus, and with His brothers.

---

[42] Acts 1:12-14
[43] Luke 24:49

Rise up!

This portrayal suggests a group that was obedient and expectant, not grumbling or questioning. They were united in prayer and preparation, following Jesus' instructions to wait in Jerusalem until the Holy Spirit came upon them. This period of waiting can be seen as a time of spiritual preparation and community building, where the disciples were getting ready to receive the power that Jesus had promised.

So, rather than expressing frustration or impatience, continue to reflect a commitment to trust and follow God's guidance, demonstrating your readiness to step into the roles that He has prepared for you.

Obedience to God: When you started, you may have thought you were stepping into your mission, but you now see that the journey was not your mission. It was your preparation. Now, here, in the promised land you were striving for, this is where you walk out your mission. Be obedient to the One Who called you.

Fellowship with God: Remain in prayer. We have a tendency to pray only when we need something and then fall out of fellowship when we get what we want. Look, your Father wants to have a relationship with you. Giving Him the silent treatment during your good times and praying only for help is almost as bad as denying His existence. Doing so is akin to trying to summon and use Him. Instead, you should surrender yourself to be used by Him. Remaining in relationship is key to receiving His guidance.

Graceful Acceptance: As people, we love to complain. We downplay our prosperity and nurture the negative as a way to relate to our fellow man. This continued practice numbs your heart from the gracious guidance of God. Let's face it, you may lose certain freedoms to walk in the responsibility of your new station. You may not be able to hang out with your pals as much as you used to, or binge a new TV series every weekend. If you've been given the tools and mission to serve, avoid complaining about receiving opportunities to use those tools. You are here because you surrendered, and in surrender, you don't fight back!

Beyond the bemoaning of sacrifices you must make in your new assignment, you may adopt the perception that your divine gifts are burdensome. When you asked God to bring you to this new station, it came with the understanding that you would be put to work. You're here to serve Him, not yourself. So, resist the urge to grumble about the workload. Viewing your tasks through the lens of your old life can make them seem overwhelming. However, you are no longer that person. You now possess a strength you couldn't fathom before.

Reflect on Paul's words in 1 Corinthians 15:10 (NIV): "But by the grace of God I am what I am, and His grace to me was not without effect. No, I worked harder than all of them—yet not I, but the grace of God that was with me." Then, ask yourself if you have truly surrendered to His all-loving, all-knowing, all-good will. This does not deny you the benefit of breaks. Physical burnout is real, but you must strive to work harder for Him than you ever did for yourself. Complaining about your workload signals to God that you lack faith in His strength within you, and it indicates you're not yet mature enough for the next level He has planned for you.

Rise up!

Embrace where you are and trust He Who brought you here. That's when you open your horizons to be more for Him than you ever imagined.

Chapter 15: Assess and Ascend Again

My call into marriage ministry was a progression. It was not an epiphany that struck me one morning, but rather a persistent tug over a couple of weeks that never let go. With my practical and analytical mindset, entering into Marriage Ministry made perfect sense. However, after reaching what I thought was my destination, God revealed a broader mission that took much longer to settle in my heart. Lynne and I operated a relationship-focused private practice for half a decade before receiving the call to open Eternal Light. During those years, I believed I spent considerable time with God—preparing sermons, earning degrees in Biblical Studies, receiving a Deaconate Ordination, and teaching Bible study classes. Yet, I later realized that my time with God lacked the expectancy of receiving a proceeding Word. I was so focused on the present that I was not truly open to the idea of moving beyond my current station.

With all my education, I began to see that my vision was limiting my potential, anchoring me as a Dating Coach, Pre-marital Counselor, and Marriage Therapist. Five years ago, I would have been thrilled to be considered a "Relationship Expert." But now? While I still love serving in these areas, I also see how struggles in other aspects of mental health affect relationships. Could we have simply expanded the practice? Sure, but that would not address the glaring issue that Christian Counseling is not as accessible as it should be. Thus, my wife and I founded a nonprofit to tackle this problem. This vision did not come to me when I started my journey; it emerged as I reached this new stage and He revealed it to me as a broader path ahead.

Assess and Ascend Again

My efforts in pruning were a resounding success. Free from those who would bring me down, I was surrounded by supportive people who believed in me and aligned with my values. This community brought peace, eliminating distractions that hindered my growth. I found inspiration in everyday living and experienced a synergy where peers helped each other excel.

During this period of growth, I sought out my sage. Unfortunately, aligning our schedules proved difficult, and we could not connect. I pressed on until I realized that perhaps God was telling me something. My sage was a safe place—he knew me, my struggles, and my heart. But was I leaning more on the man than on the Holy Spirit who speaks through him? Regardless, I surveyed the community around me and found a clear leader who had just delivered a transformative talk on apostolic expansion. His hour-long talk resonated deeply, and I spent three hours dissecting it, taking ten pages of notes. Everything he said seemed tailored for me at this pivotal moment. Despite his busy schedule, I managed to sit down with him to discuss his teachings. This conversation was life-changing. Rather than suggesting a way forward, he encouraged me to see my surroundings through God's eyes. I received a new vision for Eternal Light—not just as a Christian Counseling Clinic, but as a beacon of hope, standing in the gap for the communities we serve. Recognizing the spiritual gifts in my team, I realized God had sent us a "Dream Team" to reach the next level. With the vision expanded and the team in place, all that was left was my obedience. Let's go!

Assemble

Just as you pruned unsupportive people before starting your journey, you may have surrounded yourself with supportive people now. You've found those with skills or insight in areas you lack and have formed alliances or fellowships to share ideas and plans[44]. If you think these key individuals came by chance, reconsider. They may have been divinely placed in your life to help you reach the next stage. This is a great time to review your vision, update it if needed, and see how your circle aligns with it. You may even need a new mentor.

The call you received initially might have been limited by your capacity to understand it then. You've grown since,

---

[44] Proverbs 12:15

Assemble

and much that was once beyond comprehension is now within reach. Pay close attention to the callings on your heart and the opportunities presented. Does your vision allow for growth from where you are today? If your initial vision now seems limiting, revisit and revise it.

Revisiting your vision alone can be limiting. We often declare, "God told me to..." without confirming the call. Seek confirmation through the godly people around you, and consult your sage for insight[45]. Whether it's a board of directors, a personal advisory board, or a group of godly friends, bring your ideas to a round table for discussion. A round table is metaphorical, indicating no one person leads the conversation—everyone contributes while surrendering control to the Holy Spirit. Here are practical steps to follow:

---

[45] Proverbs 11:14

Assemble

Assemble a Strong Group: Gather people strong in their faith who preferably have an interest in your topic. The number does not matter as long as it's more than just you. Trust that God will place the right people around your table.

Invite the Holy Spirit: Start with prayer, inviting the Holy Spirit into your hearts to guide the discussion. This intentionality makes you more aware of His presence.

Take Your Time: A round table discussion can occur over time. You may talk to different people at different times. If the new calling is urgent, trust that God will make it clear by the opportunities He presents. Avoid pressing harder and faster than God is leading; accept His timeline.

Assemble

Departing from your mentor can feel like betrayal, but if that consideration becomes a real concern, reflect on Elijah and Elisha. Elisha insisted on following Elijah, demonstrating perseverance (1 Kings 19, 2 Kings 2). Simply put, he tried. He did not depart from his mentor easily. Modern-day circumstances may not allow such persistence, but if you cannot connect with your initial mentor, consider the new opportunities God presents. Seek out someone successful in your calling area and put a demand on their anointing. Persevere in your pursuit.

Once you've received insight from your trusted peers and perhaps a godly mentor, take action. You've come this far because you're a person of action. Changes in vision should expand upon what brought you here. Strategically build on what you've already built, and commit to the expanded vision. "Trying things out" can highlight a

Assemble

flakiness that leads to failure; be sure of yourself and your path. When ready, go for it!

Conclusion

Embrace Your Role as the Hero

Think of yourself as the hero in your restoration story. This perspective is not about fostering a sense of grandeur but rather about embracing humility and focus as you overcome adversities from start to finish. Heroes in stories often begin with selfish thoughts and agendas, but their character arcs lead them to use their power for a greater good. Similarly, your journey of restoration involves a transformation that requires resilience, humility, and an unwavering commitment to serving a purpose beyond yourself.

As you journey through this transformative process, grant yourself the same grace and understanding that you would offer a hero. Heroes are admired for enduring tough times, and you must recognize that your trials are a vital part of your journey. Relish being a threat to the enemy; if you weren't a threat, the enemy would not bother you.

Consider Job's story, which underscores the profound spiritual implications of human righteousness and loyalty to God. Job's unwavering faith in the face of immense suffering serves as a powerful narrative about true faith, its challenges, and the ultimate triumph of steadfast devotion. Your restoration journey, much like Job's, may offer deep insights into spiritual warfare, the integrity of faith, and the enduring power of a righteous life.

Your restoration road is not only about overcoming obstacles but also about understanding the nature of your trials and emerging stronger and more aligned with God's purpose. Reflect on the following key points as you conclude your journey and look ahead to new horizons:

Reflect on Your Journey: Take time to reflect on the challenges you've overcome and the growth you've experienced. Recognize the ways in which these experiences have shaped you and prepared you for your next steps.

Acknowledge Your Strengths: Identify the strengths and skills you've developed through your journey, and the complementary strengths in the people who surround you. Use these strengths to serve others and contribute to your community.

Stay Connected with God: Maintain a strong connection with God through prayer, meditation, and studying His

Word. Let His guidance be the foundation of your decisions and actions.

Set New Goals: As you reach this stage of your restoration, set new goals that align with your divine purpose. Let these goals challenge you to grow further and make a positive impact.

Support Others: Share your experiences and insights with others who are on their own restoration journeys. Be a source of encouragement and support, helping them overcome their challenges with faith and resilience.

As you continue on your path of restoration, remember that every step you take is a testament to God's faithfulness and your perseverance. Embrace your role as

Embrace Your Role as the Hero

the hero in your story, and let your journey inspire and

uplift those around you.

End Notes

Scripture Quotes

Key to the content of the ensuing chapters, these Biblical quotes lay the foundation of the respective step of restoration.

Chapter 1: I Believe

But the Helper, the Holy Spirit, whom the Father will send in My name, He will teach you all things, and bring to your remembrance all things that I said to you.

John 14:26

Chapter 6: Built to Bounce

The Lord is close to the broken-hearted, and saves those who are crushed in spirit.

Psalm 34:18 (NIV)

Chapter 9: The Adversary's Counterplan

And let us not grow weary while doing good, for in due season we shall reap if we do not lose heart.

Galatians 6:9

Gratitude

Thank you for receiving my personal story. I pray that the principles it highlights settle in your heart and guide you from valleys to mountaintops.

A principle we champion in our practice is the transformative power of presence. In the natural realm, we advise our counselees to surround themselves with individuals who inspire and uplift them. Spiritually, we encourage you to immerse yourself in His Word. The more time you spend with Christ, the more Christ-like you become.

I express profound gratitude for my struggles, for in them, I found the beauty of being broken. Each trial was a chiseling tool, sculpting me into a vessel for His glory. Thank you for allowing me to share my journey with you. May this testimony inspire you to embrace His plans for you, finding restoration and purpose in His grace.

www.ingramcontent.com/pod-product-compliance
Lightning Source LLC
Chambersburg PA
CBHW051143120626
46547CB00012B/923